The Legend of the Baal-Shem

MARTIN BUBER

The Legend of the
BAAL-SHEM

Translated from the German by Maurice Friedman

SCHOCKEN BOOKS · NEW YORK

CONTENTS

FOREWORD   7

INTRODUCTION   9

The Life of the Hasidim   17

    HITLAHAVUT: ECSTASY   17

    AVODA: SERVICE   23

    KAVANA: INTENTION   33

    SHIFLUT: HUMILITY   41

The Werewolf   51

The Prince of Fire   56

The Revelation   62

The Martyrs and the Revenge   73

The Heavenly Journey   79

CONTENTS

Jerusalem   82

Saul and David   87

The Prayer-Book   92

The Judgement   98

The Forgotten Story   107

The Soul Which Descended   121

The Psalm-Singer   131

The Disturbed Sabbath   139

The Conversion   149

The Return   162

From Strength to Strength   172

The Threefold Laugh   179

The Language of the Birds   185

The Call   195

The Shepherd   202

GLOSSARY   209

FOREWORD

It is fifty years since the legends of Hasidic literature cast their spell over me. Soon thereafter I began the retelling of the Baal-Shem cycle out of which this book arose. The existing material was so formless that I was tempted to deal with it as with some kind of subject-matter for poetry. That I did not succumb to this temptation I owe to the power of the Hasidic point of view that I encountered in all these stories. There was something decisive here that had to be kept in mind throughout. What that was can be gathered from what follows. But within these limits, which forbid bringing in alien motifs, all freedom remained to the epic form. Only some time after the original German edition appeared in 1907 was a stricter binding imposed on the relation which I had as an author to the tradition of the Hasidic legends—a binding that bid me reconstruct the intended occurrence of each individual story, no matter how crude and unwieldy it was in the form in which it had been transmitted to us. The results of this new relation, as they took shape in the work of three decades, were collected in the book *The Tales of the Hasidim* (Hebrew edition, 1947; English edition, "The Early Masters," 1947, "The Later Masters," 1948). Later I undertook for the first time to render satisfaction to both—truth and freedom—in the chronicle novel *For the Sake of Heaven* (Hebrew edition under the title *Gog and Magog*, 1943; English editions, 1946 and 1953).

The present revision of *The Legend of the Baal-Shem*, a product of the summer of 1954, is purely of a stylistic nature; the character of the book has remained unchanged.

MARTIN BUBER

Jerusalem, 1955

INTRODUCTION

This book consists of a descriptive account and twenty stories. The descriptive account speaks of the life of the Hasidim, a Jewish sect of eastern Europe which arose around the middle of the eighteenth century and still continues to exist in our day in deteriorated form. The stories tell the life of the founder of this sect, Rabbi Israel ben Eliezer, who was called the Baal-Shem, that is, the master of God's Name, and who lived from about 1700 to 1760, mostly in Podolia and Wolhynia.

But the life about which we shall learn here is not what one ordinarily calls the real life. I do not report the development and decline of the sect; nor do I describe its customs. I only desire to communicate the relation to God and the world that these men intended, willed, and sought to live. I also do not enumerate the dates and facts which make up the biography of the Baal-Shem. I build up his life out of his legends, which contain the dream and the longing of a people.

The Hasidic legend does not possess the austere power of the Buddha legend nor the intimacy of the Franciscan. It did not grow in the shadow of ancient groves nor on slopes of silver-green olive-trees. It came to life in narrow streets and small, musty rooms, passing from awkward lips to the ears of anxious listeners. A stammer gave birth to it and a stammer bore it onward—from generation to generation.

I have received it from folk-books, from note-books and pamphlets, at times also from a living mouth, from the mouths of people still living who even in their lifetime heard this stammer. I have received it and have told it anew. I have not transcribed it like some piece of literature; I have not elaborated it like some fabulous material. I have told it anew as one who was born later. I bear in me the blood and the spirit of those who created it, and out of my blood and spirit it has become new. I stand in the chain of narrators, a link between links; I tell once again the old stories, and if they sound new, it is because the new already lay dorman⁻ in them when they were told for the first time.

My telling of the Hasidic legend aims even as little at that "real" life which one customarily calls local colour. There is something tender and sacred, something secret and mysterious, something unrestrained and paradisiacal about the atmosphere of the *stübel*, the little room in which the Hasidic rabbi—the zaddik, the proven one, the holy man, the mediator between God and man—dispenses mystery and tale with wise and smiling mouth. But my object is not the recreation of this atmosphere. My narration stands on the earth of Jewish myth, and the heaven of Jewish myth is over it.

The Jews are a people that has never ceased to produce myth. In ancient times arose the stream of myth-bearing power that flowed—for the time being—into Hasidism. The religion of Israel has at all times felt itself endangered by this stream, but it is from it, in fact, that Jewish religiousness has at all times received its inner life.

All positive religion rests on an enormous simplification of the manifold and wildly engulfing forces that invade us: it is the subduing of the fullness of existence. All myth, in contrast, is the expression of the fullness of existence, its image, its sign; it drinks incessantly from the gushing fountains of life. Hence religion fights myth where it cannot absorb and incorporate it. The history of the Jewish religion is in great part the history of its fight against myth.

It is strange and wonderful to observe how in this battle religion ever again wins the apparent victory, myth ever again wins the real one. The prophets struggled through the word against the multiplicity of the people's impulses, but in their visions lives the ecstatic fantasy of the Jews which makes them poets of myth without their knowing it. The Essenes wished to attain the goal of the prophets through a simplification of the forms of life, and from them was born that circle of men that supported the great Nazarene and created his legend, the greatest triumph of myth. The masters of the Talmud intended to erect an eternal dam against the passion of the people in the Cyclopean work of a codification of religious laws, and among them arose the founders of the two powers which became in the Middle

Ages the guardians and vice-regents of Jewish myth: founders, through the secret teaching, of the Kabbala, founders, through the Aggada, of the folk-saga.

The further the exile progressed and the crueler it became, so much the more necessary appeared the preservation of religion for the preservation of nationality and so much the stronger became the position of the law. Myth had to flee. It fled into the Kabbala and into the folk-saga. The Kabbala indeed thought of itself as superior to the law, as a higher rung of knowledge; but it was the domain of the few, unbridgeably removed from, and foreign to, the life of the people. The saga, in contrast, lived in fact among the people and filled its existence with waves of light and melody. But it considered itself a paltry thing that barely had the right to exist; it kept itself hidden in the furthest corner and did not dare to look the law in the eye, much less desire to be a power alongside it. It was proud and glad when here and there it was called to illustrate the law.

And suddenly, among the village Jews of Poland and Little Russia, there arose a movement in which myth purified and elevated itself—Hasidism. In it mysticism and saga flowed together into a single stream. Mysticism became the possession of the people and at the same time assimilated into itself the whole narrative ardour of the saga. And in the dark, despised East, among simple, unlearned villagers, the throne was prepared for the child of a thousand years.

Groups of Hasidim still exist in our day; Hasidism is in a state of decay. But the Hasidic writings have given us their teachings and their legends.

The Hasidic teaching is the proclamation of rebirth. No

renewal of Judaism is possible that does not bear in itself the elements of Hasidism.

The Hasidic legend is the body of the teaching, its messenger, its mark along the way of the world. It is the latest form of the Jewish myth that we know.

The legend is the myth of the calling. In it the original personality of myth is divided. In pure myth there is no division of essential being. It knows multiplicity but not duality. Even the hero only stands on another rung than that of the god, not over against him: they are not the I and the Thou. The hero has a mission but not a call. He ascends but he does not become transformed. The god of pure myth does not call, he begets; he sends forth the one whom he begets, the hero. The god of the legend calls forth the son of man—the prophet, the holy man.

The legend is the myth of I and Thou, of the caller and the called, the finite which enters into the infinite and the infinite which has need of the finite.

The legend of the Baal-Shem is not the history of a man but the history of a calling. It does not tell of a destiny but of a vocation. Its end is already contained in its beginning, and a new beginning in its end.

Ravenna, 1907

The Legend of the Baal-Shem

The Life of the Hasidim

HITLAHAVUT: ECSTASY

Hitlahavut is "the burning," the ardour of ecstasy.

A fiery sword guards the way to the tree of life. It scatters into sparks before the touch of hitlahavut, whose light finger is more powerful than it. To hitlahavut the path is open, and all bounds sink before its boundless step. The world is no longer its place: it is the place of the world.

Hitlahavut unlocks the meaning of life. Without it even heaven has no meaning and no being. "If a man has fulfilled the whole of the teaching and all the commandments, but has not had the rapture and the burning, when he dies and passes beyond, paradise is opened to him, but because he has not felt rapture in the world, he also does not feel it in paradise."

Hitlahavut can appear at all places and at all times. Each hour is its footstool and each deed its throne. Nothing can

duality

stand against it, nothing hold it down; nothing can defend itself against its might, which raises everything corporeal to spirit. He who is in it is in holiness. "He can speak idle words with his mouth, yet the teaching of the Lord is in his heart at this hour; he can pray in a whisper, yet his heart cries out in his breast; he can sit in a community of men, yet he walks with God: mixing with the creatures yet secluded from the world." Each thing and each deed is thus sanctified. "When a man attaches himself to God, he can allow his mouth to speak what it may speak and his ear to hear what it may hear, and he will bind the things to their higher root."

Repetition, the power which weakens and discolours so much in human life, is powerless before ecstasy, which catches fire again and again from precisely the most regular, most uniform events. Ecstasy overcame one zaddik in reciting the Scriptures, each time that he reached the words, "And God spoke." A Hasidic wise man who told this to his disciples added to it, "But I think also: if one speaks in truth and one receives in truth, then one word is enough to uplift the whole world and to purge the whole world from sin." To the man in ecstasy the habitual is eternally new. A zaddik stood at the window in the early morning light and trembling cried, "A few hours ago it was night and now it is day—God brings up the day!" And he was full of fear and trembling. He also said, "Every creature should be ashamed before the Creator: were he perfect, as he was destined to be, then he would be astonished and awakened and inflamed because of the renewal of the creature at each time and in each moment."

But hitlahavut is not a sudden sinking into eternity: it is

an ascent to the infinite from rung to rung. To find God means to find the way without end. The Hasidim saw the "world to come" in the image of this way, and they never called that world a Beyond. One of the pious saw a dead master in a dream. The latter told him that from the hour of his death he went each day from world to world. And the world which yesterday was stretched out above his gaze as heaven is to-day the earth under his foot; and the heaven of to-day is the earth of to-morrow. And each world is purer and more beautiful and more profound than the one before.

The angels rest in God, but the holy spirits go forward in God. "The angel is one who stands, and the holy man is one who travels on. Therefore the holy man is higher than the angel."

Such is the way of ecstasy. If it appears to offer an end, an arriving, an attaining, an acquiring, it is only a final no, not a final yes: it is the end of constraint, the shaking off of the last chains, the liberation which is lifted above everything earthly. "When man moves from strength to strength and ever upward and upward until he comes to the root of all teaching and all command, to the I of God, the simple unity and boundlessness— when he stands there, then all the wings of command and law sink down and are as if destroyed. For the evil impulse is destroyed since he stands above it."

"Above nature and above time and above thought"— thus is he called who is in ecstasy. He has cast off all sorrow and all that is oppressive. "Sweet suffering, I receive you in love," said a dying zaddik, and Rabbi Susya cried out amazed when his hand slipped out of the fire in which he had placed it, "How coarse Susya's body has become that it is afraid of fire." The man of ecstasy rules life, and no external happening that penetrates into his realm can disturb his inspiration. It is told of a zaddik that when the holy meal of the teaching prolonged itself till morning, he said to his disciples, "We have not stepped into the limits of the day, rather the day has stepped into our limits, and we need not give way before it."

In ecstasy all that is past and that is future draws near to the present. Time shrinks, the line between the eternities disappears, only the moment lives, and the moment is eternity. In its undivided light appears all that was and all that will be, simple and composed. It is there as a heart-beat is there, and becomes perceptible like it.

The Hasidic legend has much to tell of those wonderful ones who remembered their earlier forms of existence, who were aware of the future as of their own breath, who saw from one end of the earth to the other and felt all the changes that took place in the world as something that happened to their own bodies. All this is not yet that state in which hitlahavut has overcome the world of space and time. We can perhaps learn something of this latter state from two simple anecdotes which supplement each other. It is told of one master that he had to look at a clock during the hour of withdrawal in order to keep himself in this world; and of another that when he wished to observe individual things, he had to put on spectacles in order to restrain his spiritual vision, "for otherwise he saw all the individual things of the world as one."

But the highest rung which is reported is that in which

the withdrawn one transcends his own ecstasy. When a disciple once remarked that a zaddik had "grown cold" and censored him for it, he was instructed by another, "There is a very high holiness; if one enters it, one becomes detached from all being and can no longer become in- *[Buddhist]* flamed." Thus ecstasy completes itself in its own suspension.

At times it expresses itself in an action, consecrates it and fills it with holy meaning. The purest form—that in which the whole body serves the aroused soul and in which each of the soul's risings and bendings creates a visible symbol corresponding to it, allowing one image of enraptured mean- ing to emerge out of a thousand waves of movement—is the dance. It is told of the dancing of one zaddik, "His foot was as light as that of a four-year-old child. And among all who saw his holy dancing, there was not one in whom the holy turning was not accomplished, for in the hearts of all who saw he worked both weeping and rapture in one." Or the soul lays hold of the voice of a man and makes it sing what the soul has experienced in the heights, and the voice does not know what it does. Thus one zaddik stood in prayer in the "days of awe" (New Year and the Day of Atonement) and sang new melodies, "wonder of wonder, that he had *[shamely]* never heard and that no human ear had ever heard, and he did not know at all what he sang and in what way he sang, for he was bound to the upper world."

But the truest life of the man of ecstasy is not among men. It is said of one master that he behaved like a stranger, ac- cording to the words of David the King: A sojourner am I in the land. "Like a man who comes from afar, from the city of his birth. He does not think of honours nor of anything for his own welfare; he only thinks about returning home to the city of his birth. He can possess nothing, for he knows: That is alien, and I must go home." Many walk in solitude, in "the wandering." Rabbi Susya used to stride about in the woods and sing songs of praise with so great ardour "that one would almost say that he was out of his mind." Another was only to be found in the streets and gardens and groves. When his father-in-law reproved him for this, he answered with the parable of the hen who hatched out goose eggs, "And when she saw her children swimming about on the surface of the water, she ran up and down in consternation seeking help for the unfortunate ones; and did not understand that this was their whole life to them: to roam on the surface of the water."

There are still more profoundly solitary ones whose hitla-havut, for all that, is not yet fulfilled. They become "unsettled and fugitive." They go into exile in order "to suffer exile with the Shekina." It is one of the basic conceptions of the Kabbala that the Shekina, the "indwelling" presence of God, endlessly wanders in exile, separated from her "lord," and that she will be reunited with him only in the hour of redemption. So these men of ecstasy wander over the earth, dwelling in the silent distances of God's exile, companions of the universal and holy happening of existence. The man who is detached in this way is the friend of God, "as a stranger is the friend of another stranger on account of their strangeness on earth." There are moments in which he sees the Shekina face to face in human form, as that zaddik saw it in the Holy Land "in the shape of a woman who weeps and laments over the husband of her youth."

But not only in faces out of the dark and in the silence of wandering does God give Himself to the soul afire with Him. Rather out of all the things of the earth His eye looks into the eye of him who seeks, and every being is the fruit in which He offers Himself to the yearning soul. Being is unveiled in the hand of the holy man. "The soul of him who longs very much for a woman and regards her many-coloured garment is not turned to its gorgeous material and its colours but to the splendour of the longed-for woman who is clothed in it. But the others see only the garment and no more. So he who in truth longs for and embraces God sees in all the things of the world only the strength and the pride of the Creator who lives in the things. But he who is not on this rung sees the things as separate from God."

This is the earthly life of hitlahavut which soars beyond all limits. It enlarges the soul to the all. It narrows the all down to nothing. A Hasidic master speaks of it in words of mystery, "The creation of heaven and of earth is the unfolding of something out of nothing, the descent of the higher into the lower. But the holy men who detach themselves from being and ever cleave to God see and comprehend Him in truth, as if there was now the nothing as before creation. They turn the something back into nothing. And this is the more wonderful: to raise up what is beneath. As it is written in the Gemara: The last wonder is greater than the first."

AVODA: SERVICE

Hitlahavut is embracing God beyond time and space. Avoda is the service of God in time and space.

Hitlahavut is the mystic meal. Avoda is the mystic offering.

These are the poles between which the life of the holy man swings.

Hitlahavut is silent since it lies on the heart of God. Avoda speaks, "What am I and what is my life that I wish to offer you my blood and my fire?"

Hitlahavut is as far from avoda as fulfilment is from longing. And yet hitlahavut streams out of avoda as the finding of God from the seeking of God.

The Baal-Shem told, "A king once built a great and glorious palace with numberless chambers, but only one door was opened. When the building was finished, it was announced that all princes should appear before the king who sat enthroned in the last of the chambers. But when they entered, they saw that there were doors open on all sides which led to winding passages in the distance, and there were again doors and again passages, and no end arose before the bewildered eyes. Then came the king's son and saw that all the labyrinth was a mirrored illusion, and he saw his father sitting in the hall before him."

Maya

The mystery of grace cannot be interpreted. Between seeking and finding lies the tension of a human life, indeed the thousandfold return of the anxious, wandering soul. And yet the flight of a moment is slower than the fulfilment. For God wishes to be sought, and how could he not wish to be found?

When the holy man brings ever new fire that the glowing embers on the altar of his soul may not be extinguished, God Himself says the sacrificial speech.

[24]

God rules man as He ruled chaos at the time of the infancy of the world. "And as when the world began to unfold and He saw that if it flowed further asunder it would no longer be able to return home to its roots, then he spoke, 'Enough!'—so it is that when the soul of man in its suffering rushes headlong, without direction, and evil becomes so mighty in it that it soon could no longer return home, then His compassion awakens, and he says, 'Enough!'"

But man too can say "Enough!" to the multiplicity within him. When he collects himself and becomes one, he draws near to the oneness of God—he serves his Lord. This is avoda.

It was said of one zaddik, "With him, teaching and prayer and eating and sleeping are all one, and he can raise the soul to its root."

All action bound in one and the infinite life enclosed in every action: this is avoda. "In all the deeds of man—speaking and looking and listening and going and remaining standing and lying down—the boundless is clothed."

From every deed an angel is born, a good angel or a bad one. But from half-hearted and confused deeds which are without meaning or without power, angels are born with twisted limbs or without a head or hands or feet.

When through all action the rays of the universal sun radiate and the light concentrates in every deed, this is service. But no special act is elected for this service. God wills that one serve Him in all ways.

"There are two kinds of love: the love of a man for his wife, which ought properly to express itself in secret and not where spectators are, for this love can only fulfil itself in a place secluded from the creatures; and the love for brothers and sisters and for children, which needs no concealment. Similarly, there are two kinds of love for God: the love through the teaching and prayer and the fulfilment of the commandments—this love ought properly to be consummated in silence and not in public, in order that it may not tempt one to glory and pride—and the love in the time in which one mixes with the creatures, when one speaks and hears, gives and takes with them, and yet in the secret of one's heart one cleaves to God and does not cease to think of Him. And this is a higher rung than that, and of it it is said, 'Oh, that thou wert as my brother that sucked on the breasts of my mother! When I should find thee without I would kiss thee; yea, and none would despise me.' "

This is not to be understood, however, as if there were in this kind of service a cleavage between the earthly and the heavenly deed. Rather each motion of the surrendered soul is a vessel of holiness and of power. It is told of one zaddik that he had so sanctified all his limbs that each step of his feet wed worlds to one another. "Man is a ladder, placed on earth and touching heaven with its head. And all his gestures and affairs and speaking leave traces in the higher world."

Here the inner meaning of avoda is intimated, coming from the depths of the old Jewish secret teaching and illuminating the mystery of that duality of ecstasy and service, of having and seeking.

God has fallen into duality through the created world and its deed: into the being of God, Elohim, which is withdrawn from the creatures, and the presence of God, the Shekina, which dwells in things, wandering, straying, scattered. Only redemption will reunite the two in eternity. But it is given to the human spirit, through its service, to be able to bring the Shekina near to its source, to help it to enter it. And in this moment of home-coming, before it must again descend into the being of things, the whirlpool which rushes through the life of the stars becomes silent, the torches of the great devastation are extinguished, the whip in the hand of fate drops down, the world-pain pauses and listens: the grace of graces has appeared, blessing pours down out of infinity. Until the power of entanglement begins to drag down the Shekina and all becomes as before.

That is the meaning of service. Only the prayer that takes place for the sake of the Shekina truly lives. "Through his need and his want he knows the want of the Shekina, and he prays that the want of the Shekina will be satisfied and that through him, the praying man, the unification of God with His Shekina will take place." Man should know that his suffering comes from the suffering of the Shekina. He is "one of her limbs," and the stilling of her need is the only true stilling of his. "He does not think about the satisfaction of his needs, neither the lower nor the higher ones, that he might not be like him who cuts off the eternal plants and causes separation. Rather he does all for the sake of the want of the Shekina, and all will be resolved of itself, and his own suffering too will be stilled out of the stilling of the higher roots. For all, above and below, is one unity." "I am prayer," speaks the Shekina. A zaddik said, "Men think they pray before God, but it is not so, for prayer itself is divinity."

In the narrow room of self no prayer can thrive. "He who prays in suffering because of the melancholy which masters him and thinks that he prays in fear of God, or he who prays in joy because of the brightness of his mood and thinks he prays in love of God—his prayer is nothing at all. For this fear is only melancholy and this love is only empty joy."

It is told that the Baal-Shem once remained standing on the threshold of a house of prayer and did not want to enter. He spoke in aversion, "I cannot enter there. The house is full to the brim of teaching and prayer." And when his companions were astonished, because it appeared to them that there could be no greater praise than this, he explained to them, "During the day the people speak here words without true devotion, without love and compassion, words that have no wings. They remain between the walls, they squat on the floor, they grow layer by layer like decaying leaves until the decay has packed the house to overflowing and there is no longer room for me in there."

Prayer may be held down in two different ways: if it is spoken without inner intention and if the earlier deeds of the praying man lie spread out like a heavy cloud between him and heaven. The obstacle can only be overcome if the man grows upward into the sphere of ecstasy and purifies himself in its grace, or if another soul who is in ecstasy sets the fettered prayers free and carries them upward along with his own. Thus it is told of one zaddik that he stood for a long time silent and without movement during communal prayer and only then began himself to pray, "just as the tribe of Dan lay at the end of the camp and gathered all that was lost." His word became a garment to whose folds the prayers that were held below would cling and be borne upward. This zaddik used to say of prayer, "I bind myself with the whole of Israel, with those who are greater than I that through them my thoughts may ascend, and with those who are lesser than I that they may be up-lifted through me."

But this is the mystery of community: not only do the lower need the higher, but the higher also need the lower. Here lies another distinction between the state of ecstasy and the state of service. Hitlahavut is the individual way and goal; a rope is stretched over the abyss, tied to two slender trees shaken by the storm: it is tread in solitude and dread by the foot of the venturer. Here there is no human community, neither in doubt nor in attainment. Service, however, is open to many souls in union. The souls bind them-selves to one another for greater unity and might. There is a service that only the community can fulfil.

The Baal-Shem told a parable: "Some men stood under a very high tree. And one of the men had eyes to see. He saw that in the top of the tree stood a bird, glorious with genu-ine beauty. But the others did not see it. And a great longing came over the man to reach the bird and take it; and he could not go from there without the bird. But because of the height of the tree this was not in his power, and a ladder was not to be had. But because his longing was so over-powering he found a way. He took the men who stood around him and placed them on top of one another, each on the shoulder of a comrade. He, however, climbed to the top so that he reached the bird and took it. And although the men had helped him, they knew nothing of the bird and did not see it. But he, who knew it and saw it, would not have been able to reach it without them. If, moreover, the lowest of them had left his place, then those above would have fallen to the earth. 'And the Temple of the Messiah is called the bird's nest in the book Zohar.' "

But it is not as if only the zaddik's prayer is received by God or as if only this prayer is lovely in His eyes. No prayer is stronger in grace and penetrates in more direct flight through all the worlds of heaven than that of the simple man who does not know anything to say and only knows to offer God the unbroken promptings of his heart. God receives them as a king receives the singing of a night-ingale in his gardens at twilight, a singing that sounds sweeter to him than the homage of the princes in his throne-room. The Hasidic legend cannot give enough ex-amples of the favour that shines on the undivided person and of the power of his service. One of these we shall set down here.

A villager who year after year attended the prayer-house of the Baal-Shem in the "days of awe" had a boy who was dull in understanding and could not even learn the shape of the letters, let alone understand the holy words. The father did not take him to the city on the days of awe, for he knew nothing. Still when he was thirteen years old and of age to receive God's law, the father took him with him on the Day of Atonement that he might not eat something on the day of penance through lack of knowledge and understanding. Now the boy had a little whistle on which he always whistled during the time when he sat in the field and pas-

tured the sheep and calves. He had brought it with him in
his pocket without the father's knowing it. The boy sat in
the prayer-house during the holy hours and did not know
anything to say. But when the Mussaf prayer was begun,
he spoke to his father, "Father, I have my whistle with me,
and I wish to play on it." Then the father was very disturbed and commanded him, "Take care that you do not
do so." And he had to hold himself in. But when the Mincha
prayer came, he spoke again, "Father, allow me now to
take my whistle." When the father saw that his soul desired to whistle, he became angry and asked him, "Where
do you keep it?" and when the boy showed him the place,
he laid his hand on the pocket and held it over it from
then on to guard the whistle. But the Neïla prayer began,
and the lights burned trembling in the evening, and the
hearts burned like the lights, unexhausted by the long
waiting. And through the house the eighteen benedictions strode once again, weary but erect. And the great
confession returned for the last time and, before the
evening descended and God judged, lay yet once more
before the ark of the Lord, its forehead on the floor and
its hands extended. Then the boy could no longer sup-
press his ecstasy; he tore the whistle from his pocket and
let its voice powerfully resound. All stood startled and
bewildered. But the Baal-Shem raised himself above them
and spoke, "The judgement is suspended, and wrath is dis-
pelled from the face of the earth."

Thus every service which proceeds from a simple or a
unified soul is sufficient and complete. But there is a still
higher one. For he who has ascended from avoda to hitla-

havut and has submerged his will in it and receives his deed from it alone, has risen above every separate service. "Each zaddik has his special way of serving. But when the zaddikim contemplate their root and attain to the Nothing, then they can serve God on all rungs." Thus one of them said, "I stand before God as a messenger boy." For he had attained to completion and to the Nothing so that he no longer possessed any special way. "Rather he stood ready for all ways which God might show him, as a messenger boy stands ready for all that his master will command him." He who thus serves in perfection has conquered the primeval duality and has brought hitlahavut into the heart of avoda. He dwells in the kingdom of life, and yet all walls have fallen, all boundary-stones are uprooted, all separation is destroyed. He is the brother of the creatures and feels their glance as if it were his own, their step as if his own feet walked, their blood as if it flowed through his own body. He is the son of God and lays his soul anxiously and securely in the great hand beside all the heavens and earths and unknown worlds, and stands on the flood of the sea into which all his thoughts and the wanderings of all beings flow. "He makes his body the throne of life and life the throne of the spirit and the spirit the throne of the soul and the soul the throne of the light of God's glory, and the light streams round about him, and he sits in the midst of the light and trembles and rejoices."

KAVANA: INTENTION

Kavana is the mystery of a soul directed to a goal.

Kavana is not will. It does not think of transplanting an image into the world of actual things, of making fast a dream as an object so that it may be at hand, to be experienced at one's convenience in satiating recurrence. Nor does it desire to throw the stone of action into the well of happening that its waters may for awhile become troubled and astonished, only to return then to the deep command of their existence, nor to lay a spark on the fuse that runs through the succession of the generations, that a flame may jump from age to age until it is extinguished in one of them without sign or leave-taking. Not this is Kavana's meaning, that the horses pulling the great wagon should feel one impulse more or that one building more should be erected beneath the overfull gaze of the stars. Kavana does not mean purpose but goal.

But there are no *goals*, only *the goal*. There is only one goal that does not lie, that becomes entangled in no new way, only one into which all ways flow, before which no by-way can forever flee: redemption.

Kavana is a ray of God's glory that dwells in each man and means redemption.

This is redemption, that the Shekina shall return home from its exile. "That all shells may withdraw from the Shekina and that it may purify itself and unite itself with its owner in perfect unity." As a sign of this the Messiah will appear and make all beings free.

To many a Hasid it is, for the whole of his life, as if this

[*33*]

must happen here and now. For he hears the voices of becoming roaring in the gorges and feels the seed of eternity in the ground of time as if it were in his blood. And so he can never think otherwise than that *this* moment and now *this* one will be the chosen moment. And his imagination compels him ever more fervently, for ever more commandingly speaks the voice and ever more demandingly swells the seed.

It is told of one zaddik that he awaited redemption with such eagerness that when he heard a tumult in the street, he was at once moved to ask what it was and whether the messenger had not come; and each time that he went to sleep he commanded his servant to awaken him at the very moment when the messenger came. "For the coming of the redeemer was so deeply implanted in his heart that it was as when a father awaits his only son from a distant land and stands on the watch-tower with longing in his eyes and peers through all the windows, and when one opens the door, hurries out to see whether his son has not come." Others, however, are aware of the progress of the stride, see the place and hour of the path and know the distance of the Coming One. Each thing shows them the uncompleted state of the world, the need of existence speaks to them, and the breath of the winds bears bitterness to them. The world in their eyes is like an unripe fruit. Inwardly they partake in the glory—then they look outward: all lies in battle.

When the great zaddik Rabbi Menahem was in Jerusalem, it happened that a foolish man climbed the Mount of Olives and blew the shofar trumpet. No one had seen him.

A rumour spread among the people that this was the shofar
blast which announced the redemption. When this came to
the ears of the rabbi, he opened a window and looked out
into the air of the world. And he said at once, "Here is no
renewal."

This is the way of redemption: that all souls and all
sparks of souls which have sprung from the primeval soul
and have sunk and become scattered in all creatures at the
time of the original darkening of the world or through the
guilt of the ages should conclude their wandering and return home purified. The Hasidim speak of this in the parable
of the prince who allows the meal to begin only when the
last of the guests has entered.

All men are the abode of wandering souls. These dwell in
many creatures and strive from form to form toward perfection. But those which are not able to purify themselves
are caught in the "world of confusion" and make their
homes in lakes of water, in stones, in plants, in animals,
awaiting the redeeming hour.

It is not only souls that are everywhere imprisoned but
also sparks of souls. No thing is without them. They live in
all that is. Each form is their prison.

And this is the meaning and mission of kavana: that it is
given to men to lift up the fallen and to free the imprisoned.
Not only to wait, not only to watch for the Coming One:
man can work toward the redemption of the world.

Just that is kavana: the mystery of the soul that is directed to redeem the world.

It is told of some holy men that they imagined that they
might bring about redemption by storm and force. In this

world—when they were so afire with the grace of ecstasy that to them, who had even embraced God, nothing appeared unattainable any longer. Or in the coming world—a dying zaddik said, "My friends have gone hence, intending to bring the Messiah, and have forgotten to do so in their rapture. But I shall not forget."

In reality, however, each can only be effective in his domain. Each man has a sphere of being in space and time which is allotted to him to be redeemed through him. Places which are heavy with unraised sparks and in which souls are fettered wait for the man who will come to them with the word of freedom. When a Hasid cannot pray in one place and goes to another, then the first place demands of him, "Why would you not speak the holy words over me? And if there is evil in me, then it is for you to redeem me." But also all journeys have secret destinations of which the traveller is unaware.

It was said of some zaddikim that they had a helping power over the wandering souls. At all times, but especially when they stood in prayer, the wanderers of eternity appeared imploring before them, wishing to receive salvation from their hands. But they also knew how to find the voiceless among the banished in the exile of a tired body or in the darkness of the elements and to upraise them.

This help is an awesome venture, set down in the midst of threatening dangers, which only the holy man can enter upon without going under. "He who has a soul may let himself down into the chasm, bound fast to the rim above through his thoughts, as through a strong rope, and will return. But he who only has life or only life and spirit, he who has not yet attained the rung of thought, for him the bond will not hold and he will fall into the depths."

But if it is only those blessed ones who can plunge tranquilly into the darkness in order to aid a soul which is abandoned to the whirlpool of wandering, it is not denied to even the least of persons to raise the lost sparks from their imprisonment and send them home.

The sparks are to be found everywhere. They are suspended in things as in sealed-off springs; they stoop in the creatures as in walled-up caves; they inhale darkness and they exhale dread; they wait. And those that dwell in space flit hither and thither around the movements of the world like light-mad butterflies, looking to see which of them they might enter in order to be redeemed through them. They all wait expectantly for freedom.

"The spark in a stone or a plant or another creature is like a complete figure which sits in the middle of the thing as in a block, so that its hands and feet cannot stretch themselves and the head lies on the knees. He who is able to lift the holy spark leads this figure into freedom, and no setting free of captives is greater than this. It is as when a king's son is rescued from captivity and brought to his father."

But the liberation does not take place through formulae of exorcism or through any kind of prescribed and special action. All this grows out of the ground of otherness, which is not the ground of kavana. No leap from the everyday into the miraculous is required. "With every action man can work on the figure of the Shekina that it may step forth out of its concealment." It is not the matter of the action, but only its dedication that is decisive. Just that which you do in the uniformity of recurrence or in the disposition of events, just this answer of the acting person to the manifold demands of the hour, an answer acquired through practice or won through inspiration, just this continuity of the living stream leads—when accomplished in dedication—to redemption. He who prays and sings in holiness, eats and speaks in holiness, in holiness takes the prescribed ritual bath and in holiness is mindful of his business, through him the fallen sparks are raised and the fallen worlds redeemed and renewed.

Around each man—enclosed within the wide sphere of his activity—is laid a natural circle of things which, before all, he is called to set free. These are the creatures and objects that are spoken of as the possessions of this individual: his animals and his walls, his garden and his meadow, his tools and his food. In so far as he cultivates and enjoys them in holiness, he frees their souls. "For this reason a man must always be compassionate toward his tools and all his possessions."

But also in the soul itself there appear those that need liberation. Most of these are sparks which have fallen through the guilt of this soul in one of its earlier lives. They are the alien, disturbing thoughts that often come to man in prayer. "When man stands in prayer and desires to join himself to Eternity, and the alien thoughts come and descend on him, these are holy sparks that have sunken and that wish to be raised and redeemed by him; and the sparks belong to him, they are kindred to the roots of his soul: it is his own powers that he must redeem." He redeems them when he restores each troubled thought to its pure source, allows each impulse intent on a particular thing to flow into the divine creative impulse, allows everything alien to be submerged in the inalienable divine.

This is the kavana of receiving: that one redeem the sparks in the surrounding things and the sparks that draw near out of the invisible. But there is yet another kavana, the kavana of giving. It bears no stray soul-rays in helpful hands; it binds worlds to one another and rules over the mysteries, it pours itself into the thirsty distance, it gives itself to infinity. But it too has no need of miraculous deeds. Its path is creation, and the word before all other forms of creation.

From time immemorial speech was for the Jewish mystic a rare and awe-inspiring thing. A characteristic theory of letters existed which dealt with them as with the elements of the world and with their intermixture as with the inwardness of reality. The word is an abyss through which the speaker strides. "One should speak words as if the heavens were opened in them. And as if it were not so that you take the word in your mouth, but rather as if you entered into the word." He who knows the secret melody that bears the inner into the outer, who knows the holy song that merges the lonely, shy letters into the singing of the spheres, he is full of the power of God, "and it is as if he created heaven and earth and all worlds anew." He does not find his sphere before him as does the freer of souls, he extends it from the firmament to the silent depths. But he also works toward redemption. "For in each sign are the three: world, soul, and divinity. They rise and join and unite themselves, and they become the word, and the words unite themselves in God in genuine unity, since a man has set his soul in them, and worlds unite themselves and ascend, and the great rapture is born." Thus the acting person prepares the final oneness of all things.

And as avoda flowed into hitlahavut, the basic principle of Hasidic life, so here too kavana flows into hitlahavut. For creating means to be created: the divine moves and overcomes us. And to be created is ecstasy: only he who sinks into the Nothing of the Unconditioned receives the forming hand of the spirit. This is portrayed in parable. It is not given to anything in the world to be reborn and to attain to a new form unless it comes first to the Nothing, that is to the "form of the in between." No creature can exist in it, it is the power before creation and is called chaos. Thus the perishing of the egg into the chick and thus the seed, which does not sprout before it has gone down into the earth and decayed. "And this is called wisdom, that is, a thought without revelation. And so it is: if man desires that a new creation come out of him, then he must come with all his potentiality to the state of nothing, and then God brings forth in him a new creation, and he is like a fountain that does not run dry and a stream that does not become exhausted."

Thus the will of the Hasidic teaching of kavana is twofold: that enjoyment, the internalizing of that which is without, should take place in holiness and that creation, the externalizing of that which is within, should take place in holiness. Through holy creation and through holy enjoyment the redemption of the world is accomplished.

SHIFLUT: HUMILITY

God never does the same thing twice, said Rabbi Nachman of Bratzlav.

That which exists is unique, and it happens but once. New and without a past, it emerges from the flood of returnings, takes place, and plunges back into it, unrepeatable. Each thing reappears at another time, but each transformed. And the throws and falls that rule over the great world-creations, and the water and fire which shape the form of the earth, and the mixings and unmixings which brew the life of the living, and the spirit of man with all its trial-and-error relation to the yielding abundance of the possible—all of these together cannot create an identical thing nor bring back one of the things that have been sealed as belonging to the past. It is because things happen but once that the individual partakes in eternity. For the individual with his inextinguishable uniqueness is engraved in the heart of the all and lies for ever in the lap of the timeless as he who is constituted thus and not otherwise.

Uniqueness is the essential good of man that is given to him to unfold. And just this is the meaning of the return, that his uniqueness may become ever purer and more complete; and that in each new life the one who has returned may stand in ever more untroubled and undisturbed incomparability. For pure uniqueness and pure perfection are one, and he who has become so entirely individual that no otherness any longer has power over him or place in him has completed the journey and is redeemed and rests in God.

"Every man shall know and consider that in his qualities

he is unique in the world and that none like him ever lived, for had there ever before been some one like him, then he would not have needed to exist. But each is in truth a new thing in the world, and he shall make perfect his special quality, for it is because it is not perfect that the coming of the Messiah tarries."

True to unique [handwritten margin note]

Only in his own way and not in any other can the one who strives perfect himself. "He who lays hold of the rung of his companion and lets go of his own rung, through him neither the one nor the other will be realized. Many acted like Rabbi Simeon ben Yohai and in their hands it did not turn out well, for they were not of the same nature as he but only acted as they saw him act out of his nature."

But as man seeks God in lonely fervour and yet there is a high service that only the community can fulfil, and as man accomplishes enormous things with his everyday actions, yet does not do so alone but needs for such action the world and the things in it, so the uniqueness of man proves itself in his life with others. For the more unique a man really is, so much the more can he give to the other and so much the more will he give him. And this is his one sorrow, that his giving is limited by the one who takes. For "the bestower is on the side of mercy and the receiver is on the side of rigour. And so it is with each thing. As when one pours out of a large vessel into a goblet: the vessel pours from out of its fullness, but the goblet limits the gift."

The individual sees God and embraces Him. The individual redeems the fallen worlds. And yet the individual is not a whole, but a part. And the purer and more perfect he is, so much the more intimately does he know that he is a

[*42*]

part and so much the more actively there stirs in him the community of existence. That is the mystery of humility.

"Every man has a light over him, and when the souls of two men meet, the two lights join each other and from them there goes forth one light. And this is called generation." To feel the universal generation as a sea and oneself as a wave, that is the mystery of humility.

But it is not humility when one "lowers himself too much and forgets that man can bring down an overflowing blessing on all the world through his words and his actions." This is called impure humility. "The greatest evil is when you forget that you are the son of a king." He is truly humble who feels the other as himself and himself in the other.

Haughtiness means to contrast oneself with others. The haughty man is not he who knows himself, but he who compares himself with others. No man can presume too much if he stands on his own ground since all the heavens are open to him and all the worlds devoted to him. The man who presumes too much is the man who contrasts himself with others, who sees himself as higher than the humblest of things, who rules with measure and weights and pronounces judgement.

"If Messiah should come today," a zaddik said, "and say, 'You are better than the others,' then I would say to him, 'You are not Messiah.' "

The soul of the haughty lives without product and essence; it flutters and toils and is not blessed. The thoughts whose real intent is not what is thought but themselves and their brilliance are shadows. The deed which has in mind not the goal but dominance has no body, only surface, no existence, only appearance. He who measures and weighs becomes empty and unreal like measure and weight. "In him who is full of himself there is no room for God."

It is told of one disciple that he went into seclusion and cut himself off from the things of the world in order to cling solely to the teaching and the service, and he sat alone fasting from Sabbath to Sabbath and learning and praying. But his mind, beyond all conscious purpose, was filled with pride in his action; it shone before his eyes and his fingers burned to lay it on his forehead like the diadem of the anointed. And so all his work fell to the lot of the "other side," and the divine had no share in it. But his heart drove him ever more strongly so that he did not perceive his sinking while the demons already played with his acts, and he imagined himself wholly possessed by God. Then it happened once that he leaned outside of himself and became aware of the mute and alienated things around him: Then understanding gripped him and he beheld his deeds piled up at the feet of a gigantic idol, and he beheld himself in the reeling emptiness, abandoned to the nameless. This much is told and nothing more.

But the humble man has the "drawing power." As long as a man sees himself above and before others, he has a limit, "and God cannot pour His holiness into him, for God is without limit." But when a man rests in himself as in the nothing, he is not limited by any other thing, he is limitless and God pours His glory into him.

The humility which is meant here is no willed and practised virtue. It is nothing but an inner being, feeling, and expressing. Nowhere in it is there a compulsion, nowhere a self-humbling, a self-restraining, a self-resolve. It is indivisible as the glance of a child and simple as a child's speech.

The humble man lives in each being and knows each being's manner and virtue. Since no one is to him "the other," he knows from within that none lacks some hidden value; knows that there "is no man who does not have his hour." For him, the colours of the world do not blend with one another, rather each soul stands before him in the majesty of its particular existence. "In each man there is a priceless treasure that is in no other. Therefore, one shall honour each man for the hidden value that only he and none of his comrades has."

"God does not look on the evil side," said one zaddik; "how should I dare to do so?"

He who lives in others according to the mystery of humility can condemn no one. "He who passes sentence on a man has passed it on himself."

He who separates himself from the sinner departs in guilt. But the saint can suffer for the sins of a man as for his own. Only living with the other is justice.

Living with the other as a form of knowing is justice. Living with the other as a form of being is love. For that feeling that is called love among men, the feeling of being near and of wishing to be near a few, is nothing other than a recollection from a heavenly life: "Those who sat next to one another in Paradise and were neighbours and relatives, they are also near to one another in this world." But in truth love is all-comprehensive and sustaining and is extended to all the living without selection and distinction. "How

can you say of me that I am a leader of the generation,"
said a zaddik, "when I still feel in myself a stronger love for
those near me and for my seed than for all men?" That this
attitude also extends to animals is shown by the accounts
of Rabbi Wolf who could never shout at a horse, of Rabbi
Moshe Leib, who gave drink to the neglected calves at the
market, of Rabbi Susya who could not see a cage, "and the
wretchedness of the bird and its anxiety to fly in the air of
the world and to be a free wanderer in accordance with its
nature," without opening it. But it is not only the beings to
whom the short-sighted gaze of the crowd accords the name
of "living" who are embraced by the love of the loving man:
"There is no thing in the world in which there is not life,
and each has received from his life the form in which it
stands before your eyes. And lo, this life is the life of God."

Thus it is held that the love of the living is love of God,
and it is higher than any other service. A master asked one
of his disciples, "You know that two forces cannot occupy
the human mind at the same time. If then you rise from your
couch to-morrow and two ways are before you: the love of
God and the love of man, which should come first?" "I do
not know," the latter answered. Then spoke the master,
"It is written in the prayer-book that is in the hands of the
people, 'Before you pray, say the words, Love thy companion as one like thyself.' Do you think that the venerable
ones commanded that without purpose? If some one says to
you that he has love for God but has no love for the living,
he speaks falsely and pretends that which is impossible."

Therefore, when one has departed from God, the love of
a man is his only salvation. When a father complained to

the Baal-Shem, "My son is estranged from God—what shall I do?" he replied, "Love him more."

This is one of the primary Hasidic words: to love more. Its roots sink deep and stretch out far. He who has understood this can learn to understand Judaism anew. There is a great moving force therein.

A great moving force and yet again only a lost sound. It is a lost sound, when somewhere—in that dark windowless room—and at some time—in those days without the power of message—the lips of a nameless, soon-to-be-forgotten man, of the zaddik Rabbi Rafael, form these words, "If a man sees that his companion hates him, he shall love him the more. For the community of the living is the carriage of God's majesty, and where there is a rent in the carriage, one must fill it, and where there is so little love that the joining comes apart, one must love more on one's own side to overcome the lack."

Once before a journey this Rabbi Rafael called to a disciple that he should sit beside him in the carriage. "I fear I shall make it too crowded for you," the latter responded. But the rabbi now spoke in an exalted voice, "So we shall love each other more: then there will be room enough for us."

They may stand here as a witness, the symbol and the reality, separate and yet one and inseparable, the carriage of the Shekina and the carriage of the friends.

Love lives in a kingdom greater than the kingdom of the individual and speaks out of a knowing deeper than the knowing of the individual. It exists in reality *between* the creatures, that is, it exists in God. Life covered and guaranteed by life, life pouring itself into life, thus first do you behold the soul of the world. What the one is wanting, the other makes up for. If one loves too little, the other will love more.

Things help one another. But helping means to do what one does for its own sake and with a collected will. As he who loves more does not preach love to the other, but himself loves and, in a certain sense, does not concern himself about the other, so the helping man, in a certain sense, does not concern himself about the other, but does what he does out of himself with the thought of helping. That means that the essential thing that takes place between beings does not take place through their intercourse, but through the seemingly isolated, seemingly unconcerned, seemingly unconnected action that each of them performs. This is said in parable, "If a man sings and cannot lift his voice and another comes to help him and begins to sing, then this one too can now lift his voice. And that is the secret of co-operation."

To help one another is no task, but a matter of course, the reality on which the life together of the Hasidim is founded. Help is no virtue, but an artery of existence. That is the new meaning of the old Jewish saying that good deeds save one from death. It is commanded that the helping person not think about the others who could assist him, about God and man. He must not think of himself as a partial power that needs only contribute, rather each must answer and be responsible for the whole. And one thing more, and this is again nothing other than an expression of the mystery of shiflut: not to help out of pity, that is, out of a sharp, quick pain which one wishes to expel, but out of love, that is, out of living with the other. He who pities does not live with the suffering of the sufferer, he does not bear it in his heart as one bears the life of a tree with all its drinking in and shooting forth and with the dream of its roots and the craving of its trunk and the thousand journeys of its branches, or as one bears the life of an animal with all its gliding, stretching, and grasping and all the joy of its sinews and its joints and the dull tension of its brain. He does not bear in his heart this special essence, the suffering of the other; rather he receives from the most external features of this suffering a sharp, quick pain, unbridgeably dissimilar to the original pain of the sufferer. And it is thus that he is moved. But the helper must live with the other, and only help that arises out of living with the other can stand before the eyes of God. Thus it is told of one zaddik that when a poor person had excited his pity, he provided first for all his pressing need, but then, when he looked inward and perceived that the wound of pity was healed, he plunged with great, restful, and devoted love into the life and needs of the other, took hold of them as if they were his own life and needs and began in reality to help.

He who lives with others in this way realizes with his deed the truth that all souls are one; for each is a spark from the primordial soul, and the whole of the primordial soul is in each.

Thus lives the humble man, who is the loving man and the helper: mixing with all and untouched by all, devoted to the multitude and collected in his uniqueness, fulfilling on the rocky summits of solitude the bond with the infinite and in the valley of life the bond with the earthly, flowering out of deep devotion and withdrawn from all desire of the desiring. He knows that all is in God and greets His messengers as trusted friends. He has no fear of the before and the after, of the above and the below, of this world and the world to come. He is at home and never can be cast out. The earth cannot help but be his cradle, and heaven cannot help but be his mirror and his echo.

The Werewolf

When death overtook the old Rabbi Eliezer, the father of the child Israel, he surrendered to it, without a struggle, the soul which had grown weary during many earthly years of wandering and affliction and longed for the fire-spring of renewal. But his dim eyes still sought again and again the fair head of the boy; and when the hour of deliverance appeared, he took him once again in his arms and held with fervent force this light of his last days, that had risen so late for him and his ageing wife. He gave him a penetrating look as if he wished to summon up the still-slumbering spirit behind the brow and he spoke,

"My child, the Adversary will confront you in the beginning, at the turning, and at the fulfilment; in the shadow of a dream and in living flesh. He is the abyss over which you must fly. There will be times when you will descend into his last concealment like a flash of lightning, and he

will disperse before your power like a thin cloud; and there
will be times when he will surround you with vapours of
thick darkness, and you will have to stand your ground
alone. But those and these times will disappear, and you will
be victor in your soul. For know that your soul is an ore that
no one can crush and only God can melt. Therefore, fear
not the Adversary."

The child read with astonished eyes the words from the
withered mouth. The words sank in and remained.

When Rabbi Eliezer had passed away, the pious people
of the community took on themselves the care of the boy
out of the love that they had had for his father. And when
it was time, they sent him to school. But he did not like the
noisy and confined place; he escaped again and again into
the forest where he delighted in the trees and the animals
and moved familiarly in the green woodland without the
least fear of night and weather. When they brought him
back with sharp reprimands, he kept still for as much as
several days under the monotonous sing-song of the teacher;
but then he slipped off as softly as a cat and threw himself
into the forest. After awhile the men who took care of him
decided that they had looked after him enough; besides
this, their trouble over the wild creature was completely
wasted. So they let him go, and he remained unchecked in
the wilds and grew up under the speechless modes of the
creatures.

When he was twelve, he hired himself out as helper to the
teacher to lead the boys from their houses to school and
home again. Then the people in the dull little town saw a
remarkable transformation take place. Day by day Israel

led a singing procession of children through the streets to
school, and later led them home again by a wide detour
through meadow and forest. The boys no longer hung their
wan, heavy heads as before. They shouted merrily and carried flowers and green branches in their hands. In their
hearts burned devotion. So great was the soaring flame
that it broke through the thick smoke of misery and confusion that presses down on the earth and flamed into
heaven. And behold, there shone forth above a resplendent
reflection.

But the Adversary swelled up with disquietude and hatred
and ascended unto heaven. Here he complained about that
which was beginning to take place below and which threatened to cheat him of his work. He demanded that he be allowed to descend and measure his strength against the pre-
mature messenger, and his request was granted.

So he descended and mingled with the creatures of the
earth. He moved among them, listened to them, tested and
weighed, but for a long time he encountered no one who
might serve the purpose of his venture. At last, in the forest
in which Israel had spent the days of his childhood, the
Adversary found a charcoal burner, a shy, unsociable fellow
who avoided other men. This man was at times compelled
to change at night into a werewolf that swept down from
afar and rushed around the homesteads, sometimes falling
upon an animal and striking terror into a late wanderer, yet
never harming any human being. His simple heart writhed
under the bitter compulsion; trembling and resisting, he lay
hidden in a thicket when the mania overtook him and he
could not subdue it. It was thus that the Adversary found

him sleeping one night, already in the convulsions of the approaching transformation, and deemed him suitable for his instrument. He thrust his hand into the man's breast, took out his heart and hid it in the earth. Then he sank into the creature his own, a heart out of the heart of darkness.

As Israel led the singing children at sunrise in a wide arc around the little town, the werewolf burst out of the still night-bound forest and rushed in among the troop with foaming mouth and livid misshapenness. The children ran in all directions, some fell senseless to the earth, others clung wailing to their leader. The animal disappeared meanwhile and no calamity took place. Israel collected and comforted the little ones; still the incident brought severe confusion and alarm to the city, especially since several of the children fell into a high fever from fright, burning in anxious dreams and moaning in the darkened rooms. No mother permitted her child on the streets any longer, and no one knew what to do.

Then the word of his dying father came back to the young Israel and now for the first time took on meaning. So he trudged from house to house and swore to the despairing parents that they might again entrust the small ones to him, for he was certain that he could protect them from the monster. None was able to withstand him.

He gathered the children around him and spoke to them as to the grown-ups, indeed more powerfully still, and their souls opened wide to him. He led them again at an early hour to the meadow, bid them wait for him there, and went alone to the forest. As he drew near, the animal burst forth; it stood in front of the trees and grew before his eyes into *took on the Adversary*

the heavens, so that it covered the forest with its body and the field with its claws, and the bloody drivel from its mouth flowed around the rising sun. Israel did not give way, for the word of his father was with him. It seemed to him as if he were going farther and farther and were entering into the body of the werewolf. There was no halt or hindrance to his step until he came to the dark, glowing heart, from whose mournful mirror all beings of the world *I - its* were reflected, discoloured by a burning hatred. He grasped the heart and closed his fingers tight around it. Then he felt it throb, saw drops run down and sensed the infinite suffering that was within it from the beginning. He laid it gently on the earth, which at once swallowed it, found himself alone at the edge of the forest, breathed freely once again, and returned to the children.

On the way they saw the charcoal burner lying dead at the edge of the forest. Those who came across him were astonished by the great peacefulness of his countenance and no longer understood the fear of him that they had experienced, for in death he appeared like a great, clumsy child.

From that day on the boys forgot their singing and began to resemble their fathers and their fathers' fathers. Growing up, they passed over the land with their heads bowed between their shoulders as their fathers had done.

*Out of relationship w/ God
Didn't defeat the Adversary —
but accepted his reflection of I - it*

The Prince of Fire

When Rabbi Adam, the man who knew the secrets of magic, was advanced in years, he was overcome by anxiety concerning who should receive his writings after his death. In them was recorded the way to the power with which he at times had grasped the machinery of fate. A son had, it is true, been born to the master, but he was only his corporal heir. That had become painfully clear to the rabbi during long years, and his will seemed to him divided and his art incomplete since they had not prevented this from happening. Once, in the summer of his strength, he had clenched his fists all night against heaven and contended with the Unnameable, who looked down on his whole daring game as on a boy's impudent venture. Later his spirit softened; he arose night after night in dreams and asked the question, "To whom, O Lord, shall I leave the source of my might?" Long had he asked in vain, and the darkness of his dream remained wordless. But one night the answer came, "You shall send it to Rabbi Israel, the son of Eliezer, who abides in the town of Okop, and you shall bestow it on him."

When in the days which followed he felt his earthly end approaching, he called his son into the seclusion of his chamber and opened the chest which hid the mystery-filled pages. Resisting the pain of bygone days, which threatened to rise again at this unseemly hour, he instructed his son, "Bring them to Israel, they belong to him. Regard it as a great favour if he shows himself ready to study with you, and remain humble at all times, for you are only the messenger, chosen to carry to the hero the sword that was forged for him by silent spirits through long ages beneath the earth."

After a short space of time the old man passed away. When he had delivered his father's mortal remains to the earth, the son arranged his earthly goods and set out with the writings of the dead man on the journey to Okop. On the way he pondered, with many trepidations, how he must go about finding this Israel who was destined to become his father's heir and his own refuge. When he reached the city the people met him with honours since he had let them know that he was the son of the wonder-working man, and he found it easy to live among them with eyes open in order to seek the chosen one. But as he looked about, no possibility presented itself to his inquiring mind other than the boy Israel, just fourteen years old, who performed small functions in the prayer house. For although the boy's actions under the eyes of all were as simple as those of other boys his age, the seeker still divined that this young child concealed a secret grace from the curiosity of the world. He decided to get nearer to him. He proceeded to the leader of the community and requested of him a quiet room in the prayer house in which he might apply himself to the holy wisdom in peace, and he asked that they might let him have the boy Israel as a servant. The leader and the others were glad to do this and regarded it a great honour for the young boy to be associated with the son of the mighty man.

But the son now pretended to be absorbed in the contents of the difficult books and not to notice what went on around him. The boy was glad of this, for he could thus continue his practice of rising from his couch every night, when one supposed him deep in sleep, and devoting himself to the Teaching. Soon, however, the young rabbi discovered this and only awaited the right moment to test him. One night, when the youth had thrown himself on his bed and immediately fallen asleep, the other got up, took a page from the magic writings and laid it on his breast. Then he hurried back to his own resting-place and held himself still. After about an hour he saw how the boy first turned himself restlessly, then how, still steeped in slumber, he seized the page, and finally how, as if held by mighty hands, he buried himself in the writings aided by the gleam of a small oil light. To the onlooker it was as if the room became brighter and larger while the boy read. Finally, Israel hid the page in his clothes and again tumbled into his bed.

In the morning the rabbi called the boy to him and disclosed to him his mission. "I give to you a thing that has only rarely lain in perishable hands," he said. "For centuries it was submerged, then it arose again to endow a human spirit with the primal stream of power. My father was the last of that short series. Now, in accordance with his decision, it belongs to you. When you linger over the writings, let my soul be the air which absorbs your words."

"It shall be as you say," Israel answered. "Yet keep silent that no one other than you and I may know of this thing."

The rabbi agreed. But in order that their secrecy might be assured, they decided to leave the prayer house and moved into a little house on the outskirts of the town. The Jews of Okop deemed it an unexpected kindness that the son of Rabbi Adam should take Israel under his protection and allow him to share in the Teaching, and since they had no other explanation, they ascribed it to the merit of his father Eliezer.

Thus it came to pass that the two entered into a solitude before which the voices of the earth grew silent.

The young Israel devoted himself entirely and without reserve to the wonderful writings and received their essence into himself. But the son of Rabbi Adam cultivated sharpness of mind. He desired to turn and weigh the strange knowledge which arose out of the old books and finally to taste the might of the magic formulae. Deprived of these things, his soul contracted and looked forth miserably out of his troubled eyes. The young Israel became aware of this and said, "What does your glance ask, my brother? What can you miss in these days?"

Then the rabbi sighed and replied to him, "Boy, would that my soul were as intact as yours! But what enters you like honey and stills your spirit eats into me like lye on wounds. In me there come and go doubts which are never

silent. There is only one who can help me, and if you would
—you who now have power over the word—let us call him,
the Prince of the Teaching."

The boy Israel was terrified. "Do not break through the
appointed time of our waiting," he cried. "The hour has
not yet come."

Disappointed, the rabbi closed up within himself. His
looks became squinted and yellow so that Israel, taking pity,
overcame his own fear and bade the rabbi prepare himself
in order that they might make ready together for the
venture.

In order to attain the kavana of the soul which was needed
to compel the Guardian of the Teaching, it was prescribed
that one enjoy neither food nor drink from Sabbath eve to
Sabbath eve nor allow access to any earthly message, but
rather spend the time in complete seclusion. So they prepared the house and barred up the doors and the windows.
They immersed themselves in the holy bath, and after that
they fasted from Sabbath eve to Sabbath eve, and finally at
the onset of the last night they stretched their souls to the
highest fervour, and Israel, with arms uplifted, called out a
spell in the darkness. But when he had finished, he fell to the
ground and cried out, "Woe, my brother! You have allowed
an error to enter our kavana. Thus a heavenly judgement
has gone forth, and already I see how the Gurdian's neighbour, the Prince of Fire, arises and poises himself for downward flight. If our eyelids sink to-night, we shall fall before
him. There is only one escape: that we remain awake and
struggle without cease till morning." They threw themselves
down and implored the spirit that they might not fall asleep.

A soft glow surrounded the house, and from it there arose enticements to rest. Toward morning the rabbi lost the power of resistance, and he leaned his head against the wall. The boy sought to arouse him, but the rabbi's already stiffening arm raised itself, and a stammer of black blasphemy broke forth from his mouth. Then the flame stabbed him in the heart, and he sank to the ground.

The Revelation

On the farthest eastern slope of the Carpathians stood a
dark, squat peasant ale-house. Its narrow front garden with
the red beets exhaled the might of the mountain, but on the
back side the slanting openings in the roof blinked across
toward broad, yellow plains which lay in light.

The small inn was quite isolated. On market days a few
people did indeed come along the road, country-folk,
Jewish traders out of the mountain villages, who spent an
hour and drank to one another's successful buying or selling; but otherwise only seldom did a hunter or traveller
stop there. When a guest came he was greeted by a slender,
brown-eyed woman and invited to sit down. Then the
woman stepped outside of the house, held her cupped hand
over her mouth and called toward the cliffs in a clear voice,
"Israel!"

In the foremost cliff, a stone's throw from the house, was

a grotto. Abundant sunlight lay before the entrance and heavy darkness on the floor. Along the sides paths ran upward into the darkness, to the height and breadth of a man, as if during the hours of night some one entered here into the kingdom of the inner earth. The cavern was silent and shut off from noises; but when the clear call of the woman came toward it, then the air, like a faithful servant, carried it to him for whom it was meant. Wherever he was, whether he lingered near the darkness at the floor of the cave or close to the entrance, he set out at the call, strode toward the yard, and stood at once before the guest in order to serve him. But a shudder gripped the heart of the guest whom he approached. Even the peasants and traders, who had known the man for many years, experienced each time afresh a feeling of awe before his glance, no matter how gentle his greeting and how careful his gestures.

He was thirty or more. The years had come to him, heavily laden with mystery, and they had passed by. He did not look back at them, he did not look forward to the ones to come. Around him was waiting: the peaks looked down on him and waited, the springs glanced up at him and waited; but he did not wait. Of these years nothing is told other than that he had long wandered in penury with his wife and later dwelt with her on the eastern slope of the mountains and served the guests. The cavern is still undestroyed; there you can see the vaulted arch and the paths.

But one day the eye of the peak, the eye of the spring was revealed to the man. He recognized that he stood in the midst of waiting. The earth burned his cavern, the silence receded from the entrance, the whispers from the walls; voices called him. Out of the arch there thundered a command, its echo resounded in the paths, the voices everywhere joined into one voice.

This morning was followed by a day, and the day by many days; the command grew great above the head of the man. He heard the step of the hour approaching out of the distance.

There came another morning when all around became clear, and the knowledge came softly up to him. The command grew silent. The Baal-Shem looked out into the world.

On this morning Rabbi Naftali was driving toward the plain. He had visited a friend to the south of the mountain, and although he had been travelling a day already, he was still full of the conversation that he had carried on with his friend. Rabbi Naftali thought of nothing other than this conversation. So the wagon came to the small ale-house on the last slope. There all thoughts grew mute in Rabbi Naftali, and he looked up startled. When he now saw the house with the bright front garden, he suddenly felt weary. He climbed from the wagon and entered the house. The woman greeted him, bade him sit down, and called toward the cliffs with her hand over her mouth, "Israel!" At once Rabbi Naftali saw the host approach with long, firm strides and smiling bow to him. He appeared to be a Jew, but he wore a peasant's garb, the short sheepskin coat with the thick, vari-coloured belt and the earth-coloured top-boots, and no cap pressed down on his long, blond hair. This annoyed the rabbi, and he was not altogether friendly when he gave him his order. The man preserved his smile and the humility of his bearing and served the rabbi so finely that it appeared almost strange how delicately the large and obviously strong man moved.

When Rabbi Naftali had rested for awhile, he called, "Israel, get the wagon ready for me, for I wish to travel on."

The host stepped out to fulfil the order, but in going he half turned and said with a smiling face, "Six days lead from the beginning to the Sabbath—why should you not remain six more days and keep the Sabbath with me?"

Then the rabbi rebuked him and bade him be silent, for frivolous talk was offensive to him. Israel kept still and made the wagon ready.

When Rabbi Naftali now drove on, he could not succeed in again recalling to his mind the conversation. While he nonetheless continued to try and would not leave off, it happened that all things became confused before his eyes. A great whirl enveloped him, and he moved along in it, in the midst of confused and confusedly revolving things. Till now, however, the rabbi had never in his life regarded the things around him; rather it had been enough for him to tolerate their presence. Now the whirl forced him to look up, and he saw the things of the world, but dislodged from their places and lost in confusion. It seemed to him as if an abyss had opened up beneath him, greedy to swallow up heaven and earth. The rabbi felt the whirl swell in his own heart, and he knew the darkness from within. But at the same moment, he saw a gigantic man in sheepskin coat and earth-coloured top-boots stride up to the wagon. The man walked light-footedly through the confusion and pushed its rushing circles gently to the side as a swimmer pushes the waves. Then he took the reins and with a strong jerk turned the horses. The animals at once galloped back the way that they had come, but with threefold speed so that in a short time they again stood at the village ale-house. Rabbi Naftali's anxiety and distress disappeared in an instant together with the confusion. He did not understand what had happened to him, but he did not question. He climbed down from the wagon and again stepped into the front garden, in whose midst stood the table now prepared for a meal. The slender woman again greeted him with a friendly and impassive face, again called toward the cliffs, and again the man of peasant appearance stood before him and bowed, not otherwise than at his first entrance.

For a long while the spell of the incomprehensible was on the soul of the rabbi. Yet hour after hour he saw around him the things in their usual manner, at rest or in ordered activity. The host, moreover, busied himself giving fodder and drink to his horses, with a noble bearing, to be sure, but otherwise exactly as any small innkeeper of the land. As a result the rabbi began to think over the occurrence, and now, as always before this day, his thoughts were again at his own command. Soon he had formed and fixed in his mind the conviction that nothing had taken place here other than a deception of his eyes weakened by the sharp air of the mountains. So he decided to remain in the lodging-house overnight and to sleep out all fatigue, but in the morning to travel on.

The next day, when the rabbi was again on the journey,

he had to laugh over yesterday's foolishness. There lay around him, beautiful and firmly interwoven, the circle of creatures, each growing and secure in its place. He imagined that he saw them now for the first time as they really were. This pleased him and he marvelled at himself. How blissful was this freedom and confidence of the creature in space! But while he wondered and rejoiced, it happened that he raised his glance to heaven and was horrified by what he saw. For instead of the light, many-toned blue or the vault pervaded by shadings of grey, familiar to him from his usual indifferent manner of looking at things, a brazen shell, hard, heavy, destitute of all joints and openings, spread itself out over the earth. As he looked down trembling, he noticed that none of the things stood in freedom and confidence, but grew, imprisoned and sickly in their places, and those that moved crept around in a wide but close and musty cage. And it seemed to Rabbi Naftali that he himself was also transfixed in an inescapable prison. He fell into a sadness out of which not even the comfort of his certainty in God was able to raise him. But his attention was unexpectedly aroused. As he looked up, he saw a man walking in the firmament. In earth-coloured top-boots he moved along the arch of heaven and touched lightly here and here the brazen ceiling. Where his finger touched it, it gave way. His finger struck breach after breach in the firmament, and the light blue streamed in. At last the whole rigid dome melted, and the flowing light again extended over the horizon, exactly as it shows itself to the eyes of men on all days. All creatures breathed deeply with relief, and even the sleeping worm turned itself as if it were throwing off fetters.

Along with all the others Rabbi Naftali too sighed out relief and breathed in freedom. He looked up to heaven to seek the man of wonder, but he had disappeared.

The rabbi turned the wagon around and drove the horses until he again stood at the ale-house. On the threshold the man whom he sought stepped up to him with the old greeting, without question in his word or gesture; but the greeting seemed to the rabbi more loving than the day before. He overcame all hesitation and spoke, "Israel, how is this that I meet you in such a manner on my way?"

Then the other looked up and smiled. The smile was like that of a sea which rests between cliffs, indulgent, smiling from its base upward, when the setting sun caresses it and speaks, "Now I give you back to yourself"—but the sea smiles and answers, "Me?" So smiled the man and answered "Me?"

The rabbi did not want to abandon his purpose, he desired to question further; but he felt that his mouth was locked, for he had been struck by the smile of the other. So he remained silent and full of questions. He could no longer go away from there, and remaining brought hour after hour new conflict to his soul. Night came and was like the day, only more lingering, and every riddle merely deepened in it. Only toward morning did his soul find release in slumber, and then it was host to a dream. The dream of the rabbi was the beginning of creation. The light separated itself from the darkness, and the firmament came into being between the waters. And it seemed to Rabbi Naftali as if the chaos out of which the world was created was his soul, and as if his soul was the faceless deep from which heaven and

[*68*]

earth sprang forth. And he felt the kneading hand of the spirit.

When he awoke and stepped out of the house, he was free of uncertainty. All appeared to him simple and definite, and he embraced the world with his eyes. He said to himself, "Now I know. There are times when the whirl rushes over the world and shatters its connections, and light and darkness are no longer separated; then the creatures lose their place and swirl hither and thither in space. And there are times when heaven holds the earth captive, and the firmament, which should only separate, transfixes and binds the creatures. But is not all this a reflection and play of time? For now I see that a good fortune hangs over the things of the world. They live together, undisturbed by whirl and spell, they walk upright through the wrath of the powers and wait. Each from its heart performs its part in the world, *uniqueness* and has joy in its work. Creation is indomitable in its felicity."

While the rabbi spoke thus to himself, he shut his eyes for happiness. But when he opened them, the first thing that he saw was the sinking downward of an enormous veil. Then the world lay before him like an abyss. Out of the abyss emerged the solar disk in silent torment. In agonized birth pangs the earth brought forth trees and plants without number, and many animals ran and flew in senseless motion. Each creature suffered because it must do what it did, could not get free, and gasped in its pain. All things were enveloped by the abyss, and yet the whole abyss was between each thing and the other. None could cross over to the other, indeed none could see the other, for the abyss was between them. This sight robbed the rabbi with one blow of what he had won in the hour before and in all hours. His heart wavered, half driven to raise itself against God, and half to suffer with God.

But as this was happening to Rabbi Naftali, he became aware of the presence of a man in the abyss, familiar to him in figure and face. The man was here and everywhere, possessed of manifold being and overspanning presence. Now his arm clasped round the body of the trees, the animals clung to his knees and the birds to his shoulders. Then lo, comfort had come into the world. For through the helper, things were joined and saw and knew and grasped one another. They saw one another through his eyes and touched one another through his hand. And since the things came to one another, there was no longer an abyss, but a light space of seeing and touching, and of all that was therein.

These were the first three days. They were followed by three others, and on each the way broadened for Rabbi Naftali. But in the little house on the mountain slope life remained as it was, and the host remained the same in walk and gesture. So the rabbi's world was like a pendulum to him, ever alternating between the wonder of the far and the wonder of the near. He dared no word more, no questioning glance; he lived and waited.

Thus the Sabbath evening drew near. The host spoke the greeting to the holy bride with simple and humble words and conducted the meal faithfully after the manner of pious, unlearned men. For a while Naftali glanced at the others and at his host and expected he knew not what salvation. But nothing happened. He was still waiting when the host had already blessed the table and waited still when he arose to extend his hand to the guest and wish him peace for this night and for all of his life.

In the night the rabbi found no sleep. It seemed to him as if here and now the wonder of the far and the wonder of the near must flow together.

In the middle of the night the command came to him, soundless and without form. He arose and went. Then he was already in the other chamber and saw: The chamber was filled with flames up to the height of a man. They rose dull and sombre, as if they were consuming something heavy, hidden. No smoke ascended from the fire, and all the furniture remained uninjured. But in the middle of the fire stood the master with uplifted forehead and closed eyes.

The rabbi saw further that a division had taken place in the fire which gave birth to a light, and the light was like a ceiling over the flames. The light was twofold. Underneath it was bluish and belonged to the fire, but above the light was white and unmoving and extended from around the head of the master unto the walls. The bluish light was the throne of the white, the white rested on it as on a throne. The colours of the bluish light changed incessantly, at times to black and at times to a red wave. But the light above never changed, it always remained white. Now the bluish light became wholly fire, and the fire's consuming became its consuming. But the white light that rested on it did not consume and had no community with the flame.

The rabbi saw that the head of the master stood entirely in the white light. The flames which leaped upward on the body of the master turned to light, and every little while the amount of light increased. At last all the fire became light. The blue light began to penetrate into the white, but every wave that penetrated itself became white and unchanging.

The rabbi saw that the master stood entirely in white light. But over his head there rested a hidden light that was free of all earthly aspects and only in secret revealed to the beholder.

The rabbi fell to the ground. Then he knew the man and the goal of the six days.

When the morning came, they celebrated the holy Sabbath together.

The Martyrs and the Revenge

When the might of Bilbul took possession of the city of Pavlitz and the lie came rushing along in triumph, the Jews from all the places in the region fled abroad before the threatening destruction. But some pious old men would not let themselves be induced to leave there. "This people is like a long pent-up sluice," they said to their souls. "It wants to crush us in order to taste its power. But how long have not we been like a pent-up sluice and could not serve God as we wanted to! From the time of our birth our lives have been a disturbed and desecrated service of God. For here we have no place in which to rejoice in God, and we breathe an air which is not the Lord's. Once the matza was the work of our fields and the strength of our hands lived in our fields and served God. But now the matza comes to us out of the earth of strangers who are our enemies. Once the etrog was the delight of our gardens, and our joyous heart-beat served God. But now the etrog comes to us like a guest from a distant land that we shall not behold. In this distant land the roots of our prayers have remained. Now we speak the words, but can rootless words grow upward to God? It is not given to us to serve the Lord with our lives. So we wish to serve Him with our death and endure for the sanctification of His name."

So they spoke to their souls, allowed themselves to be taken captive, and waited joyfully until they should be killed.

One, however, did not remain with them. That was the rabbi of Karitzov. When he was young, he had begun a book which told how one could serve God with one's life. He had lived rigorously and sternly and had put all his power, all his longing, and all his thought in the book. If he dreamed and willed anything, he took his dream and his willing in his hand like a stone and laid it on what had been built before, that his edifice might grow upward to God. So one part of his book was slowly joined to the other. But everything was so arranged in it that an ascent from lower to ever higher rungs of service prevailed. Whenever the rabbi set to work to treat of a new rung, he prepared himself in great ardour of soul and lived in collectedness until he went into his chamber to write. There he sat and did his work, and none dared call him and remind him of food and drink or sleep until he had completed his treatment of that rung. Nor did he speak to anyone of his book.

When the Bilbul now drew near, the rabbi communed with his own soul. A profound dialogue went on in the silent chamber throughout many hours. The book had developed up to the highest rung, but of this rung he had not yet begun to treat. Now it lay on the table, yet he did not look at it. At last, however, his glance came and rested on the book. He arose, took the book and prepared to flee to Wallachia.

When he came to Mesbitz on his way, the Baal-Shem bid him remain with him until he should send him away. So he remained with the Baal-Shem. "The holy men shall be saved," the latter said to him, and repeated it time after time. But on the evening before the Sabbath a letter came to the rabbi. It related that the pious men had been tortured with all manner of death pains, and that they had passed away in torment and in great joy to the sanctification of the Name. When the Baal-Shem had seen the letter, he went to speak the afternoon prayer and trembled, and whoever beheld him had to tremble. And one spoke to the other, "When now the hour comes to receive the Sabbath, joy will certainly return to him. For no matter what has happened to him, not yet has he received the Sabbath without joy." But the hour came and the Baal-Shem received the Sabbath with great trembling and held the goblet in a trembling hand. Then he went into the little room in which he slept and laid himself on the ground, his face to the floor and his arms outstretched; and he lay thus a long time. Finally, when the servants and the guests were waiting for him, his wife came into the room and spoke, "The lights are already going out."

"Let the lights go out and send the guests home," he replied. So she went, but he still lay on the ground.

The rabbi, however, could not endure the waiting any

longer. He went to the room of the Baal-Shem and listened. It was very still in the room. He went to the door and looked through a crack in the door into the darkness. Thus he stood until midnight. Then a great gleam of light illuminated the room. The Baal-Shem greeted each of the martyrs by his name and called, "Blessed be he who now comes!" Then he spoke to them, "I charge you that you take revenge on the enemy. On the senator who let you be put to the rack. On the servant whose hand was ready for your torment. On the people whose mouth was ready to exult over your suffering."

Then there sounded through the room a dark chorus which was yet like one voice, "We implore you, do not let this word pass over your lips a second time."

But he repeated, "I charge it to you."

And again the holy men said, "We suffered our death gladly."

But the Baal-Shem stood in the midst of the light and called, "For the beating and stabbing, for the slow murder, for the shame through their hands, for the kicks of their feet, for the humiliation and abasement, for the mocking and jeering, for the servitude of the centuries, for the necessity of becoming bad, take revenge."

There was a quiver in the voice of the chorus. "We implore you," it said, "do not let this command proceed from your lips a third time. Know that on this evening you have disturbed the Sabbath of the worlds. A great anxiety was everywhere, and we did not know its source. We ascended to higher spheres, there too was the anxiety, and we did not know how to explain it. When we came to a very high sphere, we were told, 'Descend quickly, dry the tears of Rabbi Israel Baal-Shem.' So we want to tell you of what has happened to us.

"As we were being tortured, the evil urge came over us and wanted to force our spirits to bow, but we thrust it away with both hands. Still he succeeded in touching a thought in us with a finger-tip, and he made a sign on the thought. Because of this thing it was decreed that we must come for a moment into the chasm of Gehenna and in it suffer a moment long the need of the world. All the pain that we had suffered died away and became a mere trifle before this suffering. When afterwards we came into the Garden of Eden, we said, 'We want to take revenge for the servitude of the centuries, for the necessity of becoming bad that has given the evil urge power to touch our thoughts. For our lives' desecrated service of God, we would take revenge.' 'If you want to take revenge,' we were told in reply, 'you must enter once again into bodies, return to the earth, and live a human life to its end.' We then reflected. 'We praise the Lord, blessed be He,' we said, 'and thank Him that we have persevered for the sanctification of His name and that for a moment long we have suffered the need of the world in the chasm of Gehenna. But if we return to the world where we have no place in which to rejoice in the Lord, and where we breathe an air which is not the Lord's, it might happen that we shall become worse and the might of evil will be heightened. We do not want to return.' Thus we spoke. Therefore we implore you that the command not go forth from your lips a third time."

Then the Baal-Shem remained silent. The gleam of light vanished from the room, the darkness filled it again. The Baal-Shem lay speechless on the ground. But the rabbi of Karitzov did not complete his book. Indeed, no man knows what became of it.

Thought his book more important —

The Heavenly Journey

By day he serves the creatures. Messengers come travelling on the winds, petitioners ascend from the ground. Surging together from the mouth of all living things, the voice of their sufferings pushes forward to him.

He receives the call and bestows the answer. Incessantly he gives his gift, his powerful comfort. Under the touch of his finger the wounds of the world are healed.

By day he serves the creatures. But at evening his soul frees itself. It does not wish to rest with its indolent comrades. It slips off place and duration like a pair of manacles. Pushing off from the land with its feet, it assays flight, and heaven admits the emancipated soul.

In heaven there is no place and duration, only way and eternity. Each night the soul travels farther on the way, deeper into eternity.

But a night comes when a world-wall rises up before the

soul and obstructs its path and its view. Boundless as was the flight is now the hindrance. The way vanishes. A finger has extinguished the light of all the stars and the promise of all the heavens. Where the vanished way had been, a dark wall stretches into the night.

The wall has a face, enormous and shadowy. The soul recognizes it: it is the face of the life which it left behind in the evening and into which it will return in the morning as into a waiting bed.

But on the far side of the wall a sound awakens, a great voice in the darkness.

The voice speaks:

"Soul, longing soul, which wishes to guard itself and to lose itself, which demands both, existence and infinity, meaning and mystery, at once!

"Here is the boundary. Here is the altar of the world. Here no soul passes unless it sacrifices itself. For the name of this place is: God's choice.

"Up to here both existence *and* infinity hold good. Here begins the one. Soul, which has attained this far, choose!

"Detach yourself from this earth and I shall open to you. Or turn back your flight. He who has touched me does not return."

The voice grows silent.

The soul stands for a moment as it listens to the words that are dying away, then it speaks the answer,

"I detach myself from—"

At this moment a woman on the earth is bending over a bed in which lies the body of a man. She gazes, she touches questioningly the paling temple of the reclining man. Then she screams, "Israel!"

The cry rises to heaven in steeply ascending flight. Before the moment is concluded, it stands at the end of the way which the soul has achieved in many nights and lays its light hand on its shoulder.

The soul breaks off its words and looks around. It does not speak further. It lays its arm around the neck of the messenger and turns back its flight.

This was the last journey of the master in heaven.

Jerusalem

It happened at times that voices out of the depths called to the Baal-Shem at night, and his ear became awake and attentive though sleep still encompassed his senses. He distinguished then with great clarity how out of the distances the cry from the mouth of many ancient things was on its way to him, and a single murmur of terrible woe visited his bed. The voices reached his heart and awakened it. But they came from all too far away, and his heart did not understand the meaning of their words. It could only surmise the great need out of which they spoke, and from this time on, both during the days and during the nights, it was strongly shaken by the impact of these cries.

One night, however, the voices were quite close to the master's ear. He recognized them and knew from where they came to him. It was the old land that spoke to him out of the shame of its degeneration. It was the vineyard, now become a fallow steppe, the walls buried beneath the earth, the submerged metal that reverberated under the burden of the rubble, the petrified slope that had once borne the shining forest, and the dried-up spring. They cried out of their final need, for they sensed that from one moment to the next, from one breath to another, their sleep would slip imperceptibly into death if the liberating hand did not come.

"Come and do not delay," the voices spoke to the Baal-Shem. "You are the awaited one. The brook will run, the forest rise up, the vine bear fruit, the rock will clothe itself. Come and lay your hand on us!"

From that night on the Baal-Shem was certain in his soul that he must arise and go to the land. He stretched himself upward and cried to God, "Give me leave, Lord, and respite. Unloose that with which you hold me bound here in order that I may go into your land which calls me."

But God spoke powerfully to him and answered, "Israel, it is my judgement over you that you remain in your place and do not appear in my land."

Many nights the Baal-Shem lay in torment. The voices were at his ear and the word of the Lord was on his heart. But the lamentation of the voices rode like a storm in the air, and it was a movement like that of a great dying, as on the day on which Jerusalem fell. Then the appeal of the dying earth triumphed over the word of heaven, and the master made ready to travel to Jerusalem.

It was the first night in which they laid themselves to rest under a strange roof, the Baal-Shem and Rabbi Zvi the scribe, his disciple. During that night the voices returned to the place from which they had come. When they reached home, they heard a great whispering, the old earth trembled under their greeting, and each thing raised itself up and listened.

"Arise, you sleeping ones," the voices called. "Prepare yourselves, for your deliverer is on the way!"

With a deep breath the body of the earth shook off its ancient sleep. Each thing uttered the call of life, and a powerful joy resounded in the night. The sunken treasure blossomed, sword and offering-cup, the exhausted waters rose up with a roar, the sap of the corn and the vine circulated anew.

The Baal-Shem strode indefatigably forward, but brightness and joy were no longer with him. He remained silently absorbed in his thoughts; and when Rabbi Zvi spoke to him of the wonderful goal of their journey, the master gave hardly any other answer than a forlorn sigh. For a matter weighed heavily on his heart, and it became heavier as they went on their way. This was the voice of God which had had to grow mute before the yearning and now kept silent, but remained ever present and did not withdraw from his heart. Often at night there came, wholly within, a plaintive sound without words to which he, awakening, had to listen and listen in himself. Yet every morning he carried the growing burden farther on the journey.

Thus he left city and country behind him, the familiar and the strange. The moon had already changed above him many times when, after a day of going astray, he came at evening to the coast of the sea which separated him from his goal. But there was neither house nor habitation here as far as the eye could see, no sail on the water, only strand, shimmering and boundless, the breaking of the water on the sand and a tepid night with a mild light in the heavens. Then on the earth, which still exhaled the glow of the vanished day, they threw themselves down, to rest and to await the morning which would show them the way to a navigator.

In the middle of the night the master found himself with his fellow-traveller on the high sea in a tiny boat without rudder, with only a sail over it, flaming red and yellow. But the little ship was tossed hither and yon by the storm, and neither sky nor land was to be seen on any side; only water roared unfettered to all distances. The Baal-Shem looked about him, but there was nothing other than the water's deathly isolation. He looked within himself, but there everything had forsaken him, wisdom and mastery. He found his soul empty. A great weeping overcame him. Then he threw himself down next to his companion. But while he lay, a miserable thing, a voice arose very gently and began to speak. At first it spoke softly and mysteriously, then gradually the voice of God swelled and engulfed in its sound the raging of the sea with all its mighty clamour.

At dawn the Baal-Shem and Rabbi Zvi lifted themselves from the sand, with hair, faces, and clothes wet through like those of men whom the sea has washed up on the shore. They did not speak, each avoided the eyes of the other and turned away; and without a word they walked back together the way they had come in the evening.

After many hours of wandering—the sun had dried their

damp clothes—the rabbi looked by chance at the master and perceived the old holy light on his countenance.

During the night in which the Baal-Shem struggled with the abandonment on the water and with the abandonment in his soul, the land which had called him lay in expectation. The voices of those who were buried alive spoke forth out of the earth and questioned the voices in the air, "What do you hear?"

Then spoke their sisters in the air, "A storm rages, and on the turbulent waters strives the man who shall deliver us."

Some time passed, then the voices of the earth again questioned, "Is he nearing the land?" And the answer came, "The Word is over him."

Still more time vanished, and once again ascended the question, "What do you hear?" And like the rustling of earth-weary wings the answer came back, "We hear out of the distance the step of the departing one." Then the old earth veiled its face and closed its eyes. Each thing returned to the place of its rest. Silence covered all of the land.

Above the silence a call came to life, broke through it and dispersed it. "You will not die, my friends," the call spoke to the land. "Earth of the Lord, you will awaken and live. Do not be wrathful with him whom you have called. He is born as one who shall return. The hand of the Lord is over his roots to bring him back in his time, to bring him back in your time, O my friends."

NOT TIME

Saul and David

The Baal-Shem had not long returned from the uncompleted journey before the men began to gather around him
in order to receive help and healing from the blessing of
his hand and the counsel of his mouth. They sat at his
table, and to each the general word of the master seemed
a secret that was meant for his ear alone and for no
other's.

But it happened now and then that the Baal-Shem paused
in his speech and for a time grew silent and detached, his
eyes unseeing and unfocused, and remained thus among his
friends. At such times his followers would wait patiently
until the master's senses should have returned to him. When
this took place after a while, the holy man appeared exhausted as if an unknown force had nearly compelled the
fountain of his soul to run dry. He found a friendly word
for each of his guests, to be sure, but soon he would

arise and go into his chamber in which he then shut himself
for many hours.

The disciples often talked among themselves of this occurrence, yet no matter how much they sought, they never
found the meaning of the strange happening. Then it came
to pass once that Rabbi Wolf, the joyous, who never gave
access to any anxiety and who was always confident in the
love of the master, approached him about this matter and
received an explanation. From thence we know how it happened. What took place later, however, was reported by
the man himself through whom the event was concluded.

In the time of the Baal-Shem there lived in the city of
Kossov a rabbi who attacked him out of a dark, powerful
spirit. This quarrel, however, was ancient and had its origin
in the great days of the kings. It was reported that, as a
heritage and pledge of the times, Israel the son of Eliezer,
whom we call the Baal-Shem, bore in his blood the soul
which had once forsaken David the King when his youth
was shattered and lust overtook him. But the Rabbi of
Kossov incorporated within himself the soul of Saul, the
prince of dreams. It happened from one time to another,
therefore, that he would be seized by a hidden anger which
he harboured within himself the whole day. Then from time
to time he sent forth his maddened soul to approach the soul
of the Baal-Shem and insinuate that they might measure
their strength against each other. Thus the Baal-Shem was
at times forsaken by his soul which went forth to battle.
Time after time it sprang up sharply from the struggle like
clear flames against the sky, while the soul of the other
weakly flickered.

[*88*]

To be sure, the Rabbi of Kossov never spoke against the master; yet he could not expel the shadow which came over his face when all tongues bore living witness for the Baal-Shem. This did not remain hidden from the disciples who adhered to the rabbi. They suffered to see his features so distorted and often tried with goading talk to incite him to open conflict. "Tell us, sir," they said, "how it happens that all the people come to this man and sing his praises with transfigured tone as if touched by a grace? Is it perhaps because of the fact that no one has ever come yet who is great and simple enough in spirit to shatter his arts? Go to him that he may measure himself against you, then shall we and everyone behold the truth."

For a long time the rabbi resisted these words, for he was proud and honest with himself and knew his enemy well. Since his disciples did not cease to press him however, they finally succeeded in influencing his soul. One day he prepared himself and his followers for a trip and travelled unto Mesbitz to the Baal-Shem. When they entered his house, he came to meet them and greeted the rabbi. The latter bowed and returned the greeting, and it was as if two heroes of olden times gave to each other welcome. They appeared removed from their comrades and were themselves no longer aware of anything else than each other. The disciples remained in the forecourt, but the two men went into a chamber, and as the door fell shut behind them, the waiting band felt as if they were separated from them by something other than a wooden door.

The two stood eye to eye, and between them was again, as in the olden time, the twofold flaming of the hearts. But soon there was only wrath in the rabbi. He devised complex speech for himself and hurled it against the Baal-Shem that he might become entangled in it and succumb to him. But it fell to the earth without strength. The conversation between the two wandered here and there for awhile, but the Baal-Shem rested like a child in his certainty. Then the rabbi asked, "Is it true what they say, Israel, that you know every thought of the sons of men?"

The master answered, "It is true."

Thereupon the other asked again, "Then are you aware of what fills my thoughts at this time?"

"You know," said the Baal-Shem, "that the thoughts of men do not usually rest but rather circle here and there. Bind now your thoughts to one thing, and I shall name it for you." The rabbi did this, and the Baal-Shem said: "It is the secret name of God to which your thoughts cleave."

When the other recognized that the saint had gazed into his spirit, a feverish exasperation seized him, and he cried, "This you can know without magic vision. I must keep the name of God before me at all times, and when you bid that all my thinking cling to one thing, what remains to me besides this last, this one? I have little regard for your art."

But the Baal-Shem persevered in his mildness. "Has not God many names?" he said. "But I speak to you of the one unutterable name." When he saw, however, how the glance of the rabbi quivered and resisted, he stepped before him. Out of his eyes there now broke forth unfettered a stream of love, and he said, "This is what you thought, Nachman: 'Shall I forever remain imprisoned in the power of the Name? Will this tyrannical Word forever coerce me? The ages have sunk down and have ascended again and the spirit still holds me in chains. Whither hast thou flown, last of the pure days, when I went through the land of Benjamin with joyful shoulders, a head taller than all the people? Day of sun, day of freedom, thou hast never come again. But thy brother remains, he who succeeded thee; he remains with me with his oil glass and the name of the Lord. He encircles my neck when I lie down, he clasps my ankles when I spring up from my bed. He has given me wrath to drink, and he has given me madness to eat. He guides my sword against my body: daily I fall upon it and die.' This is what you thought, Nachman: 'Shall I forever remain imprisoned in the power of the Name? How then if I should free myself and again become as I was then, before I came into the city where the man of the Lord was!' But I say to thee, Nachman, my friend, thou friend of God, dost thou wish to make thy heart free from thy breast? See, thou hast recognized thyself—art thou still imprisoned? See, thou hast recognized thyself—dost thou not feel thy will cradled in the will of God? Take the burden of the ages in thy hands— has it not already disappeared? Greet the day which enchains thee—art thou not already freed?"

"You have spoken the truth, Israel!" said the rabbi. Then he bowed, spoke the word of peace, and departed at once with stilled spirit.

The Prayer-Book

On the two high holidays which are called the days of awe,
that is, the festivals of New Year's and the Day of Atonement, the Rabbi of Dynov, when he stepped before the holy
ark to pray, used to open the great prayer-book of Master
Luria and lay it before him on the stand. Thus it lay open
before him all the time of his prayer, but he did not glance
at it or touch it. Rather he let it lie there in the face of the
ark and before the eyes of the community, large and open
so that the strong, unfaded black of the letters on the broad,
yellow background was visible from all sides; and he stood
very erect before it in his consecration, like the high priest
sacrificing before the altar. All eyes must needs glance at it
ever again, but none of the Hasidim dared to speak of it.
Once, however, a few of them emboldened themselves and
asked the rabbi,

"If our master and teacher prays out of the book of

Master Luria, why does he not look inside it from page to page according to the order of his praying; and if he does not pray out of it, why does he open it and why does it lie before him?"

"I will tell you," the rabbi replied, "what happened in the days of the holy Baal-Shem, may his memory be a blessing.

"There lived in a village a farmer with his wife and his small son. The lord of the manor had a great affection for the quiet man and granted him many privileges. Nevertheless bad years overtook him. A poor harvest was in the next summer ever again followed by a poorer one, and so his destitution grew until the huge grey billows closed over his head. He had stood firm before every trouble and every deprivation; he could no longer look misery in the eyes. He felt his life grow weak and weaker; and when his heart at last stood still, it was like the dying away of the swing of a pendulum which no one had noticed while it became steadily slower and whose stopping now came over one as something sudden. And as his wife went with him through pleasant and evil fortune alike, so now also she went out of life with him. When his grave was ready, she could no longer force herself to continue. She looked at her little son and still could not force herself, and so she laid herself down and tried to convince herself that she would not yet go to her death.

"Little Nahum was three years old when his parents died. They had come from a great distance, and no one knew of any relatives. So the lord of the manor took him for himself, for he was well pleased by the boy with the narrow, blossom-white face glimmering forth out of the red-gold locks. Soon the child's manner made him ever dearer to him, and he reared him as if he were his own child.

"The boy grew up and was instructed in all knowledge. But he knew nothing of the faith of his parents. To be sure, the lord of the manor did not conceal from him the fact that his father and his mother had been Jews; yet when he spoke to him of it, he added, 'But I have taken you, and now you are my son, and all that is mine is yours.' Nahum understood this well; but what was said to him about his parents seemed to him to belong to those stories that the servant girls told him of wood-spirits and water-sprites; it was altogether wonderful and incomprehensible to him that he himself had something to do with such a story.

"One day he came unexpectedly upon an out-of-the-way chamber of the house in which all kinds of discarded things lay piled one on top of the other. These were the possessions which his parents had left behind them. There were strange things which he did not recognize. There was a remarkable white shawl with long black stripes. There was an embroidered forehead cloth of a splendid nature. There was a powerful, many-sided lantern. There was a rich, many-branched spice-holder coming together into a crown, around which a thin mist of air still hovered. And there was a great, heavy book bound in well-worn dark-brown velvet, with edges of beaten silver and silver clasps. These were the things that his parents had not been able to give up, not even with the approach of misery.

"And now the boy stood and looked down at the book. Then he took it and carried it carefully into his room, hugging it tightly in his arms. Then he loosed the clasps and opened it, and the broad, black letters inside whirled round before him like a band of tiny comrades. As he lost himself now in looking at it, he beheld two eyes opposite him, tearless but full of pain. And Nahum knew that this was the book out of which his mother had prayed. After that he kept it hidden during the day, but each evening he fetched it out of its hiding-place, and by the light of a lamp, and preferably even by the living light of the moon, he looked at the strange letters until the eyes of his mother emerged.

"Thus the days of judgement drew near, the fearful and merciful days. Out of all the villages the Jews travelled toward the city in order to stand before God in the community of the people and in order to allow each one's guilt to vanish in God's fire along with the guilt of the thousands. Nahum stepped to the door of the house and saw the carriages hurry by, saw men and women in them in holiday clothes. He felt as if all these men were messengers to him, and as if they only passed quickly by him because he did not call to them. So he called to one of them and asked him, 'Where are you travelling, and what is this time for you?'

"The man who was addressed replied, 'We travel in order that in a large group we may ask God for forgiveness of our wrong.'

"From this hour on the boy's world was illuminated for him.

"Thus passed the ten days of repentance and the day before the holiday of Atonement was there. Again the boy saw the Jews travel the streets of the city from out of the villages. And again Nahum asked one of them, 'What brings you to the city?'

" 'This is the day for which we have waited,' the man replied, 'the Day of Atonement in which the Lord receives his children into the home of his grace.'

"Then the boy hurried into his room, took the book with the silver edges in his arms and ran out of the house into the street, ran until he came to the city. In the city he turned his steps to the prayer house and entered it. It was the hour when the Kol Nidre was spoken, the prayer of absolution and of holy freedom. He saw the group, standing in long, white shrouds, bow and again lift themselves up before God. He heard them cry out to God, out of all the hidden depths of the soul toward the light. The boy stood among them, bowed and again lifted himself up before God. And since he was aware that he could not pray in the language of the others, he took his mother's book, laid it on the desk and called out, 'Lord of the world! I do not know what to pray, I do not know what to say—but here, Lord of the world, you have the whole prayer-book.' He laid his head on the open book and weeping conversed with God.

"It was on that day, however, that the prayers of the community fluttered on the floor like birds with lame wings and could not soar up. The spirit of the men who prayed was troubled and despondent. Then came the word of the boy and took the prayers of all on its pinions and carried them to the lap of God.

"But the Baal-Shem knew of this happening, and he spoke the prayer with great joy. When the holiday was over, he took the boy to himself and taught him the pure and blessed truth."

Thus the Rabbi of Dynov told his pious. "I also do not know what I should do," he said, "and how I can fulfil the intention of the early men of prayer out of whose mouths the prayers came. Therefore, I open before God the book of Master Luria, the venerable, and give it to Him with all the will that is in it and all the meaning."

The Judgement

It happened once—it was on the fourth day of the week
and about the first hour of evening, when the sun has just
vanished from our sight—that the Baal-Shem left his house
to make a journey. He had not spoken of where he was
going to any person, either disciple or friend, so that the
goal and meaning of this trip remained a mystery for all his
followers, even for those who accompanied him. This time
too he drove a great stretch of the way in a short space
of time; for it is known to all, indeed, that place and
time were not fetters to the will of the master as to one
of us.

About midnight the Baal-Shem stopped in a strange village before the house of a tax-collector and innkeeper, in
order to rest there for the hours of the night which remained to him. It became apparent that the host knew
neither the Baal-Shem nor any of his followers, but, as is

not seldom the case among people of this profession, he was nonetheless curious to know to what station his guest belonged and to what end he had undertaken this trip. While he offered the master and the others a late meal and made their beds for them, he exchanged questions and answers with them. In reply to the innkeeper's inquiries the Baal-Shem gave him to understand that he was a preacher and that, having been informed that on the coming Sabbath the wedding of a rich and distinguished man was going to take place in Berlin, he wished to be there at that time in order to officiate at the ceremony.

When the host heard this, he remained silent and perplexed for awhile and then said, "Sir, you mock my inquisitiveness! How can you travel that stretch of road in the time which remains to you! Indeed, if you did not spare horse and man, you might perhaps be able to be there for another Sabbath, but never for this one."

The Baal-Shem smiled a little and replied, "Do not concern yourself about that, friend; I am sure of my horses. They have already done many good pieces of work for me."

Soon after that he lay down to rest along with his followers. But the host remained awake in his bed the whole night long, for the strange man and his business appeared to him all too remarkable. Yet there was something in the glance of the man which did not allow the innkeeper to believe that he was a joker or even a fool. The longing came over him to see this thing through to the end. He therefore thought of a clever pretext to offer the strange preacher his company. In fact, a great deal of business occurred to him that he might take care of to some advantage in Berlin. Then he decided to talk this over with his guest in the morning.

When the master and his followers had risen from bed, the host went to him and reported his wish, and the Baal-Shem agreed. On the other hand, he showed no especial hurry to be on his way, looked around the house tranquilly, spoke a prayer with his followers, and finally bid the host prepare still another large meal. This they ate and remained then in conversation while the innkeeper ran up and down out of unrest and curiosity.

When the day had already descended, the master commanded that the wagon be made ready and the horses hitched to it. They travelled away, and soon the night came over them. The Baal-Shem and his followers sat silent. This appeared rare and strange to the mind of the innkeeper, and it seemed to him that this was a trip the like of which he had never yet taken. There was nothing else but darkness. At times it felt to him as if they rolled deep underneath the streets of men through mysterious passages in the earth, and then again the way that they took felt to him so light and transparent that it seemed as if they floated in the air. They encountered no noise, no people, no animals, no places. The innkeeper could not control his thoughts. Everything in him and around him appeared to have dissolved into something fleeting and transitory.

Suddenly it seemed to him as if the air around him became denser, the first light dawned, he felt beneath him again the shaking of the wagon on the floor of the earth, a dog barked in the distance, a rooster crowed, a hut lay to one side in the dawn light. They travelled thus for awhile, the morning became clear, and when the last mists vanished before the sun, the innkeeper saw before him a great city. Barely a quarter of an hour passed by before they reached Berlin.

The master selected a modest inn which stood on the outskirts of the city, in that neighbourhood where low houses lay in their little gardens almost as in the country. Then he sat down with his disciples to breakfast in an arbour in front of the house. After they had eaten, they remained together in prayer and speech. The innkeeper who had made the trip with them thought of the statement of the preacher that he was travelling to Berlin to the wedding of a great man and that to-day was the day of the ceremony, and he could not understand how the Baal-Shem could remain so tranquil instead of going to associate with the guests in the house of the bridegroom. Still perplexed by the events of the night and yet already pricked by this new question, he approached the master. But when he prepared to open his mouth, the Baal-Shem raised a cheerful countenance, and the innkeeper saw thereon the merry mockery with which the latter, in great kindness, smiled at his restless soul. Then the courage for the question deserted him, and he took leave in order to wander about a little in the strange city.

He was not under way more than an hour when he saw that on every side the people stood together in order to share a piece of news with one another and to discuss it. So he went up to one of them and asked what might have happened to cause the people to forget their affairs. He received this information: in the house of a rich Jew, whose wedding was to have taken place that very day, the bride had suddenly passed away in the morning after she had worked with great joy until midnight getting her finery ready, had made the preparations for the feast, and had spent the rest of the night in restful sleep. Also she had in no way been sick or weakly, but was known to all as a beautiful and strong young creature.

The house of the bridegroom was pointed out to the innkeeper. He entered there and found the wedding guests standing in distress and confusion around the dead girl, who lay on the bed, pale but undeformed. The doctors, who appeared to be still troubled about her, were just now taking their leave of the master of the house, expressing with some embarrassment the opinion that she who was dead must now remain dead. The bridegroom stood motionless; his face wrapped round with grief as with a grey veil. This and that one among the guests came up to him and whispered words meant to comfort him, but the man remained mute as if he had not heard. Then the innkeeper also ventured to go up to him, and he told him of the unusual manner in which he had travelled such a great way that night with the strange preacher. He gave it as his opinion that the wonder-worker who could make this journey would probably also know how to do much more that was out of the ordinary, and he advised the master of the house to go to him and confide his suffering to him. The bridegroom gripped his hand, held it fast and requested to be conducted to the inn of the Baal-Shem. He went before the master, told him the whole of the painful event, and bade him come to the bed of the dead. The Baal-Shem went with him immediately to the lifeless bride and gazed long at her silent face.

Everyone grew still and waited for his word. But he

turned from the waiting men and said to the women, "Prepare quickly the winding sheet for the dead and carry out
your customs without delay." To the bridegroom he said,
"Bid men go to the cemetery where you bring the dead
of your house to rest and prepare an abode for this one
too." Then the bridegroom sent there and had a grave dug.
"I shall go with you in the funeral procession," the master
said. "But take the wedding clothes and the gown that you
yourself have selected for this day and bring them to the
grave." When everything was arranged, they laid the corpse
in an open shrine and carried it out. The Baal-Shem walked
first after the coffin, and many people followed him with
bated breath.

Before the grave the Baal-Shem commanded that the
dead should be laid in the grave in the uncovered coffin so
that her face looked up freely to heaven and could be seen
by all. He also ordered that no earth should be thrown on
her. He gave instructions to two men to stand near him and
await his orders. Then he stepped up to the open grave,
leaned on his staff, and let his eyes rest on the face of the
dead. Thus he stood without moving, and those who saw
him observed that he was like one without life, as if he had
sent his spirit forth to another place. Everyone stood in a
wide circle around the grave. After awhile he motioned to
the two men. They drew near and saw that the countenance
of the departed had reddened with the breath of life and
that breath came and went out of her mouth. The Baal-
Shem bade them lift her out of the grave. It then happened
that she stood up and looked around her. Then the master
stepped back and commanded the bridegroom that he

should instantly and without speech clothe the bride in her veil and that he should lead her to the bridal canopy and not recall the incident by any word. The bridegroom, however, asked that it be the master who should bless the marriage.

So they led the veiled girl into the house under the canopy. But when the Baal-Shem raised his voice and spoke the marriage blessing over the pair, the bride tore the veil from her face, looked at him and cried, "This is the man who acquitted me!"

"Be silent!" the Baal-Shem rebuked her. The bride grew still, and before the people could realize what was happening, the master had left the house.

Later, when all the wedding guests sat at the meal and the shadow of the past event began to fade, the bride herself arose to tell her story.

Her bridegroom had already been married once, and it was as a widower that he had desired her for a wife. However, the first, dead wife had been her aunt who had taken her in and cared for her as an orphan and allowed her to grow up near her in the house. Then it happened that the wife became ill and there was no help for her, and she herself knew well that her time had now come to an end. It weighed heavily on her spirit that when she should have been dead for a little while, her husband, who was not yet old, might possibly raise up another in her place. And as she thought about this, she realized his choice would fall on her young relative, who knew all the affairs of the great house so well and was pleasant to behold and who would be before his eyes every hour of the day. And because she herself had loved her husband very much and was disquieted over the short time which had been granted her to be at his side, she was very envious of the young creature. As she felt her last hour slip away, she called both of them to her bedside. And when they who loved her saw her pining away so, their souls overflowed with sorrow. She exacted a solemn promise from them never to marry each other. To the two of them, who suffered over the dying woman, this promise did not seem difficult and they gladly gave it.

But then the dead woman was carried away, and her place was empty. Even her shadow faded from the room, and there were now only the living, and all around them was life. They looked in each other's eyes every hour, and soon they understood that they could not let each other go. Then they broke their oath and pledged themselves to each other.

But on the morning of the wedding, when the house was full of joy and no one thought of the dark days when one now dead had dwelt there in sadness, the will of the dead woman came back to its abode, demanded that its violated rights be restored, and sought to kill the fortunate woman. Now, at the bidding of the strange power, the life of the bride was torn away from her body, which lay there stiff. Then her soul struggled mightily over the bridegroom with the soul of the dead.

When she was carried to the grave, both of their souls came before the judgement. It was the voice of a man which administered justice over them, and they fought before him over the decision. The voice gave the verdict, "You dead, who no longer have a share in the earth, let go of her. For behold, justice is with the living. This woman and this man bear no guilt. They must do what they did not want to do in order to still the need of their souls." And since the dead would not desist from oppressing the bride, the voice cried out to her, "Let go of her! Do you not see that she must go to the wedding? The canopy is waiting!" Then the bride awakened to life, allowed herself to be lifted out of the grave and clothed in her veil, and still slightly stunned, she followed the women to the canopy.

"But," she said to the bridegroom and to the guests when she had finished her tale, "when the preacher spoke the blessing over us, I recognized the voice which had pronounced judgement over me."

The Forgotten Story

When the body of the Baal-Shem was almost consumed by the fire of his soul, he called all his disciples to him. He had already stretched himself out on his last bed; his head was raised a little, resting on his left hand, and his face, during the whole time that he spoke, was turned fully toward his followers. His glance rested steadily on him to whom he spoke. He told each one of the group how he should lead his future life and in which spirit he should live it.

Among his disciples was one who served him and was always near him. His name was Rabbi Simon. The Baal-Shem called him last of all and said to him, "Friend, it will be your destiny to travel about in the world and to visit all places where Jews dwell. There you will go into the houses and tell stories; you will speak of me and set forth with faithful words what you have seen and experienced in all your days of living with me. And what men place in your hands as a reward for your living word, that will be your livelihood."

Discontent arose in the heart of Rabbi Simon. To be sure, he loved more than anything else in the world to speak of the master and to reproduce the master's words with his own lips. But how might it benefit him to go about like a beggar, with no house, not even the smallest, to call his own, an eternal wanderer, a guest at strange hearths? He was not able to bring himself to remain silent but had to allow his drop of bitterness to flow into the death of his master. So he said in an undertone, "What will be the sense of that? I shall become wandering and vagabond and the poorest pilgrim here below."

Then the Baal-Shem comforted him and said to him, "Your road will reach a good end, friend."

When it happened soon afterwards that the master entered into the Eternal, the disciples thought with love of fulfilling that which his will had destined for them. Rabbi Simon put on a traveling garment, walked away from there, and went from city to city to narrate to all Jews the stories of the holy Baal-Shem. He won honour from this and found an easy living. And since he was still young and could allow his eyes to rove with an unburdened spirit, he took a liking to the beautiful roads which led over the multi-coloured earth, and he no longer felt any fear in coming and going.

Thus two and a half years passed by. Then he met an old man who came from Jerusalem. This man gave him to understand that in Italy, in a city whose name he gave him, there resided a rich Jew who bore in his heart an astonishing love for the holy Baal-Shem. His whole spirit was filled by him, and all his endeavours centred on hearing about the master. Then Rabbi Simon told himself that this Jew in Italy must be the right man to hear of the wonderful happenings of which he knew how to speak. For his words concerning the exalted man had, indeed, passed over many foolish spirits and by many frivolous ears, so that he now felt a desire to tell them to a genuine listener who would open his heart to him.

He bought a horse and prepared himself for the journey. It was seven months before he came to the city of the rich man, for he had to remain long enough at each place on the way so that through his story-telling in the houses he might earn the money for the expenses of his further travel. Immediately after his arrival in the city he went into the house of a Jew and asked after this man who cherished so great a respect for the Baal-Shem. Then the people told him that the Jew of whom he spoke had come to the city as a stranger about ten years before. Already at that time he had brought with him great wealth. Once, after he had spent a few months there, the last of a princely line died. The dead man's palace and all his property surrounding it fell to a distant relative in Rome. This relative did not want to leave his hereditary home so he expressed the wish to sell the inherited property. It was the foreign Jew who then came forward and paid in pure gold the tremendous purchase price. And all the Jews of the land were happy beyond all bounds that the foreign man should be housed among them so splendidly, for there was a pious and kind life-spirit in and above him. On the Sabbath his palace was open to every honourable Jew. In the broad halls stood the Sabbath tables in a radiance of linen and silver; since the fall of the holy city, the day of the Lord had probably nowhere been celebrated so resplendently as here. At each of the three meals of the Sabbath, the host always had a story of the holy Baal-Shem recited to him and his guests, and everyone was received in honour who had something to say of the man rich in grace. And his reward was also beyond all custom: on the day after the festival, the great Jew himself presented it to the narrator in well-coined gold.

When Rabbi Simon learned this, he sent to the palace and had it announced there that a servant and disciple of the holy man had arrived in the city. The steward of the house came immediately, took him away, and, with many marks of esteem, conducted him to the castle where a number of beautiful and comfortable rooms were assigned to him.

Meanwhile, the news circulated among the Jewish people in the city itself, indeed in the whole surrounding country, that a disciple of the Baal-Shem had come. On the Sabbath all those who were curious to hear hurried to the table of the hospitable man in a greater crowd than ever before. When the songs of the first Sabbath meal had solemnly and ardently resounded among the pillars of the hall, the master of the house raised his face and turned it toward Rabbi Simon, who read therein a request and an expectation. In a gentle voice the great man invited him, if he deemed his house worthy, to speak of the great master for the comfort of their souls.

Rabbi Simon sat upright in his chair, laid his arms on the

carved arm-rests, and opened his mouth to allow the image of the wonderful man to arise in respectful words. He was used to the reports of the life of the Baal-Shem coming to his lips of themselves. But as he sat there now, expecting the speech to take shape in his mouth, an icy coldness suddenly came over him from within, the words froze on his lips, he stiffened and paled. As from behind a veil, he saw many eyes hanging on his mouth; he opened his lips, but the sound was still-born. He was pained by the silent demand on all faces, which remained pitilessly turned toward him. He collected all his strength in order to set the image of the master before his soul; he thought of the city of Mesbitz, its houses and walls and gardens and all the little things that were so familiar to him, but his thoughts did not change into an image. Confused and ashamed, he broke out in tears.

Lifting his eyes, he saw that everybody regarded him as a deceiver, treacherously left in the lurch by the lying spirit. Only the master of the house looked at him lost in thought and full of kindly understanding and said, "We shall wait until morning. Perhaps your memory will come back to you."

Rabbi Simon lay the whole night in tears and waited for the image of the Baal-Shem to visit him. But his mind remained deserted. When he appeared at the Sabbath morning meal everyone looked past him. But the master of the house spoke to him again, "Perhaps you can tell us a story now."

Then Rabbi Simon spoke to him and swore that this night of forgetfulness into which his thoughts had sunk was no empty and accidental thing, but surely was decreed for him for some meaningful purpose by a power arising from a deep source. The rich man answered, "Let us wait until the third meal."

Rabbi Simon perceived a humble smile on his countenance. But the pain and shame which visited him were much too great for him to reflect on this within himself. At the third meal too his memory did not return to him. But he fortified himself with love and accepted all with a faithful heart, for in his innermost being he now divined that all this had to take place in order that old chains might be loosened.

The Sabbath passed, however, and nothing had changed. The day after, Rabbi Simon took his leave. The rich man let him go with eyes sunk in sorrow and presented him with a handsome gift that should compensate him for the long journey and his many wants. He also gave him a comfortable travelling carriage with servants in order that they might bring him to the border of the country, from where he would more easily be able to get along by himself. The guest descended and sat himself in the carriage. Everything was ready and the coachman was just urging on the horses when Rabbi Simon felt as though a flash of light had travelled like lightning through his body. When he was able to collect his thoughts, he realized that a great story of the holy Baal-Shem stood intimately before his soul with the clarity of a picture. He gave himself up for a while to the fervent delight that had overcome him at the moment of grace; then he bid the coachman turn back the carriage which had already gone several streets' distance from the palace. When they reached the house, he sent a servant to the master and had him announce that Rabbi Simon had returned for he had recalled a story of the holy master. The master received him, but the trembling expectation in his countenance escaped Rabbi Simon, who saw and felt nothing but his story. "I bid you sit before me," said the master, "and inform me of the occurrence which you have recalled at this hour." Rabbi Simon told him this story:

"It happened once about the time of the first spring, just before the days in which the Christians celebrate their Easter, that the holy Baal-Shem passed a whole Sabbath in gloom. He went about the house deeply absorbed and anxious, as if his soul had forsaken him for a dangerous battle and he awaited its return. After the third meal, which he ate in silence, he ordered that the carriage be made ready and the horses hitched to it. His melancholy had lain over the house and his followers like a threatening, dark thundercloud. With his command to prepare for the drive out, a sigh of relief swept through the room for everyone knew that it was by travelling thus into the country that what had before been knotted always became straightened out.

"This time there were three of his followers to whom he granted the privilege of taking part in the trip, and I was among them. We drove the whole night, and, as often before, no one knew the goal of the journey. As the morning light climbed slowly upward, we entered a great city. The horses slackened their furious course, and, as if checked by an invisible hand, suddenly halted before the door of a dismal house whose side lay in a narrow street while its gable-end seemed turned toward a broad square. The gate was closed, the windows covered by shutters, the street lay deserted and silent. The master bid me descend and knock. I knocked for a long time in vain: finally, I put into my knocking all my longing for rest, and the sombre, shut-in house reverberated with my blows. Then a small door which was set in one of the giant side wings of the gate was opened from within.

"Before us stood an old woman with a troubled face out of which reddened eyes stared at us. Suddenly she shouted at us, 'What drives you to come here just to-day! What, do you not know then that you are on the way to the slaughter-house?' And since I looked at her uncomprehendingly, for it seemed to me that we had come on a madwoman, she drew us into a doorway and said, 'Now I see that you are strangers and are not familiar with the customs of our city. This is how it is: there has been here for several years a Christian bishop, a proud, unbending man who is the deadly enemy of the Jews. He has now commanded that all the Jews that are found on the streets on the day before their Easter holiday should be seized and martyred in revenge for their Messiah. Therefore, we are on our guard on these days and hide ourselves in the very interior of our houses. They know that well, so now they want to draw lots to determine on which of our people the torment shall fall. But you,' she shrieked, and pushed us toward the carriage, 'you who are strangers here they will not spare! You do not know the people of this city, they are ravening beasts when their blood is enkindled. Hurry, try to reach the next place and wait there until the end of this unhappy day before you come here to do your business!' Thus shouted the old woman and raised her hands on high.

"But the Baal-Shem paid no attention to her; he shoved her to one side, entered, and bid us open the gate and hide

the carriage and horses in the stall and the supplies which
we brought with us in the house. He stood and looked on
tranquilly while everything took place according to his
word. Then he bade us close the gate and door once more,
and we stood in the great, dark entrance-hall. The master
beckoned to us and led the way, climbing several steps on
the staircase of carved wood. He opened the door and we
entered a stately room which was elevated a small height
above the level of the earth. I stood for awhile before my
eyes took in the room, for although outside, meanwhile, the
bright morning had ascended, the chamber lay in darkness.
The window shutters were closed, and heavy curtains were
drawn together over them. After looking around a little
I became aware of the fact that the room concealed many
men. They had hidden themselves noiselessly in the corners
as if through their anxiety they had lost consciousness. The
whole household might well have been gathered there.

"Meanwhile the old woman had followed us from the hall
weeping and now reproached the Baal-Shem on the grounds
that his entrance might bring down misfortune on her
house. But he did not answer her. Instead he measured the
room with great strides and then halted by one of the
windows that looked out into the open through a semi-
circular bay. He calmly stretched out his hand and shoved
the curtains back; then he opened the window and the
wooden shutters behind it and now stood with his whole
figure against the open frame. The morning light and a fresh
breeze streamed in. The old woman no longer dared to
speak out loud, but she entreated the master with desperate
gestures to close the window again and step back. Since, for

all that, he paid no attention to her, she finally sank silently to the floor next to the others.

"The opened window that now afforded us a free view did not look out on the narrow street through which we had come, but rather on that great square to which the gable side of the house belonged. In the midst of it I saw a church of white stone which sent upward two towers. Just opposite our window, on the outer side of the walls, a pulpit was constructed. About thirty stone steps led up to its summit. When the master had opened the window, only a few men stood in the square; but they increased in number from one minute to the other and now stood in a thick crowd around the pulpit. Now the voices of many bells boomed above us. Outside among the men a movement was perceptible, a shoving and pushing; then there opened up in the dark crowd a broad, light street and there appeared in splendid procession, with banners, lights, and clouds of incense, the bishop under his silver canopy. Everybody became still and waited while he ascended the steps of the pulpit in his glittering, brocaded gown. Then he sank into a silent prayer to prepare himself for his sermon, and the whole crowd kneeled noiselessly.

"The master stood steadfast in the open window and looked out. Then he spoke in a clear voice into just this silence, 'Simon, go outside and say to the bishop, "Israel, the son of Eliezer, is here and sends for you."' When the people who were in the room with us heard these words, consternation overcame them, and they allowed themselves to forget the dread which had formerly driven them to hide in the corners. They sprang out, surrounded the Baal-Shem and protested against what he had bid me do. But he stood as if their words did not reach his ear and his understanding, looked at me meaningfully and said, 'Go, Simon, go quickly and do not be afraid!'

"And I, who had hesitated for the length of a thought, now recognized my master as before and went through the crowd to the pulpit, and no one spoke even a word or laid a finger on my garment. I strode up half of the stairs, then I halted and addressed the bishop in the Hebrew tongue, 'Israel, the son of Eliezer, is in that house. He sends for you that you should come to him.'

"Then the bishop answered me in the same tongue, 'I know of his presence. Say to your master that I shall appear before him immediately after the sermon.'

"I turned around, went through the crowd in the square, and entered the house. The people with whom we stayed had crept to the closed window to peer at the place and see what would become of me. They saw that I came through the crowd to the pulpit unharmed, held discourse with the bishop as I had been bid to do, and returned again safely. Then they understood that there must be something great about our master, and as I entered the room I perceived how they surrounded my master and asked his pardon. He, however, listened imperturbably to my message as if he and I were alone in the house. When he had heard me, he smiled a little and said to me, 'Return, go once more to the pulpit and say to the bishop, "Do not be a fool. Come at once, for the man who summons and invites you is Israel, the son of Eliezer."' I did as he bid me and marched again to the pulpit. When I stepped onto the square, the bishop had just begun to preach. I climbed up and tugged a little at his mantle. Then he halted and looked at me, and I repeated the words of the Baal-Shem. I noticed how his face changed colour at my speech; then he turned to the people and said, 'Be patient for a little while. I shall return.' He followed me over the square through the crowd in his gold- and flower-embroidered robe, the high gold cap on his head, and thus he entered the house and stepped before my master, the holy Baal-Shem.

"They both went into a separate room, closed the door behind them and remained there for two hours. Then the Baal-Shem alone came out. He was greatly comforted, in his eyes shone the glory of God. He ordered us to prepare carriage and horses, and we drove away from there.

"I do not know what took place between the bishop and our master. Even the name of the city I do not know to this day, for the Baal-Shem did not inform us of it at that time or later. I know only that it was a great thing that the holy man had effected when he came out of that closed room, for he looked like a cherub from the heavenly hosts. After his death I failed to make inquiries concerning that event, for it had gone completely out of my mind soon after our return, and to-day for the first time, just as I had left this house, I recalled it again."

When Rabbi Simon ceased speaking, the rich man stood up, raised his hands to heaven and praised God. "My friend," he said to Rabbi Simon, "blessed be thy coming and blessed be each of thy words. I know that the truth came out of your mouth. I shall inform you of that part of the occurrence which must have remained dark to you.

"That bishop whom you summoned was I. I recognized you as soon as you entered my house. Once I was a Jew filled with the true wisdom and a hallowed soul was mine. Then the alien spirit won power over me so that I fell from faith. Soon I won the high regard of the adherents of my new creed. I took the holy orders of their church and climbed ever higher in office until I ruled as bishop over all the souls of this land. But my hatred against my own people was great. In the nights, to be sure, when my soul was defenceless, the shame of the apostate came over me. In the day-time, however, when I was fortified, I took revenge for the unrest of my nights and nourished all the malice in the souls of my community against the children of the people that I had disowned.

"My Jewish ancestors, however, had been an honourable race, proud of their faith. They had performed great service before the Lord, and many a one of them had sealed the holy covenant with his blood. The peace of their eternity was disturbed through my misdeeds. They sought out the Baal-Shem and bade him have mercy on my fallen soul. Then the holy man entered my dreams and struggled in them with the evil spirit that possessed me. The two of them were mighty warriors, and I was torn hither and thither between them like a wretched leaf in a storm. But on that Sabbath of the Jews which preceded the Christian Easter holiday, the spirit of the holy man was by my side day and night. He had already conquered my will; in the night I determined to flee the next morning—to leave everything and return to the people of my childhood. But with the day doubt arose in me. The bells called me, the waiting crowd surrounded the church, and the servants laid the golden garments on my shoulders. I was no longer able to renounce all this power over the human spirit, and I mounted the pulpit. Then the holy man sent you to summon me. But I wanted to speak my sermon first, for I thought to strengthen my will through my own words and through the inflamed hearts of those who surrounded me, in order that I might be able to persist in my defiance before the master. You called me a second time, then all resistance deserted me and I followed, as a child in the twilight obeys the call of its mother.

"I came to the master, he struggled over my soul and won it. He showed me the way whereby I could be redeemed from my guilt, and I became a penitent from that hour on. I confessed my error before the king and all the people; then I left the country. I came here, passed my years in the purification of my soul and awaited the divine absolution. For know that the Baal-Shem had proclaimed to me, 'When once someone appears before you from a foreign land and tells you your story, that will be a sign of liberation from the fetters of your deeds.' When you came now and all recollection of events was removed from your thoughts, I understood that this was for my sake because I had not yet completed what I must do. Therefore, I plunged anew into the depths of devotion. But now that you have recalled my story, I know that I have been delivered.

"But you, my friend, will now have a fixed abode and will never again be a wanderer on the earth. For all that is mine I will divide with you, from whose mouth the word of deliverance came to me."

The Soul Which Descended

Among the many childless wives who came to the Baal-
-Shem with requests for a miracle, there was one woman
who came back regularly every little while to weep at the
feet of the master and to bind the need of her life to his
heart. She appeared and vanished without many words, yet
with a flame burning in her eyes. When the Baal-Shem saw
her for the first time among his visitors, she was a lovely,
fresh young creature. But in the course of the years, during
which she often returned in her penetrating, silent manner,
her countenance turned yellow and became haggard, as
if everything in her had been consumed by the great
wish.

Once more she bowed her slender head before the master,
her eyes moist with silently flowing tears, imploring with
this one respectful gesture. But this time he laid his hand on
her head and remained pensively silent for a while. Then he

sighed deeply, looked down on her, and said softly, "Go home, woman. Within a year you will bear the son whom your soul desires!"

For seven years the master did not see her. But then one day he again found her among the group of visitors, leading a beautiful boy by the hand. "Master," she said, "behold here the child that was born to me according to your word. I offer him to you, for know I tremble because of his nature which does not appear to have been born out of mine, as his body out of my body." The Baal-Shem looked at the child and it seemed to him as if he had never seen anything so gracious and proud as this little creature in his shabby clothes. The boy also looked up, but not shyly or trustingly after the manner of children. With great seriousness, he sank his eyes in those of the master.

The Baal-Shem lifted the child in his arms and asked the woman, "How can your heart allow you to part with him for whom you have striven with God all the years of your youth?"

"Master," she answered, "when the boy opened his eyes for the first time and looked at me with a strange glance, as if from far away, my poor heart tightened in astonishment, as if he were not of my blood. Then as he grew larger, he looked beyond our little house with his far-away eyes and lived with us like a guest and not like one of the family. Although he was also quiet and good and caused me little trouble through the needs of his body, yet he gave me anxiety all the time, Master; for in his little face there is always a patient waiting and listening. Then the courage to bring up this child deserted us altogether, for it seemed

to us that he who will be a guide for him must see farther than we two poor people. Therefore, I offer him to
you."

The Baal-Shem nodded silently and let the woman go.
But he took the boy into his household and allowed him
to grow up near him. The boy was in a position of such
great favour that it astonished all who saw it. When he grew
up, many rich men would gladly have brought honour to
their house by marrying a daughter to him, and it happened
at times that one among them spoke to the master about
this. But he paid little attention to them, and smiling gently
he turned them off. Thus the opinion grew among all that
none of these matches was sufficiently splendid for his
adopted son. Hence their respect for the master led them to
forget their desire.

It happened one day that the Baal-Shem bid a trusted
disciple go to a distant city and there seek a man whose
name he told him. He bid him give this man a letter which
he placed in his hands. The messenger went as he was commanded to do, came after two weeks' wandering to the
designated place, and inquired after the man in the houses
of the pious. But it appeared that not a soul knew the name.
Day after day passed by without any news coming to the
seeker, and he was becoming discouraged. One evening he
met an old, bowed and needy Jew who was selling a basket
of fresh garden fruits. When he chanced to ask his name,
it turned out that this must be the man for whom the letter
of the Baal-Shem was intended. After the messenger had
discovered this, he handed him the letter; but it appeared
to him strange that the holy man could have anything

important to communicate to this man, so mean and foolish in appearance.

But the tradesman did not know how to read at all, and so the messenger opened the letter and read it to him. It was written therein that the Baal-Shem asked the poor man's third-born daughter as a wife for his adopted son, and her name and age were given. Then the Baal-Shem explained that he was willing to take care of the trousseau and the wedding out of his own funds. He was also willing to be of further assistance to the father in case he was in need in any way. "Are you satisfied?" the messenger asked the old man.

"Ah, sir," he said, and laughter broke out all over his careworn face, "how should I not be satisfied? Do I not have a houseful of daughters who run barefoot and fight among themselves over the rare bites of food? But this child that the exalted one desires as a wife for his boy is much too refined for my poverty. She performs her daily work as if she moved in a dream and speaks in such a way that I, a simple old man, hardly know what she is saying!"

On the next day the messenger, the old man, and his child departed to go to the Baal-Shem. When they had arrived at the house of the master, he received the father and his daughter with love and showed so much kindness to them that they rose up in cheerfulness like plants in the morning light. Soon the house prepared for the marriage. The Baal-Shem himself spoke the blessing over the young people. When the meal had come to an end and all who sat at the empty tables were joyful and festive at heart, the Baal-Shem, almost as if unintentionally and turned only toward his neighbour, began in a soft voice to tell a story. From his expression, however, everyone guessed that this thing of which he began to speak came from the fountain-head of his vision and touched on the meaning of this holy day. So they became attentive and broke off all activity, countenance and being turned toward the master. The bridal pair clasped hands and listened.

The story ran thus:

"There once ruled in a distant land a powerful king with far-reaching territories. This king was very sad for many years because his wife had borne him no son.

"Once he spoke with a magician about this desolation of his life. The latter listened thoughtfully to him, smiled mysteriously and then spoke, 'My lord, there is only one thing to do: we must compel the powers above by the passionate onslaught of wishing souls. It may be, however, that your sadness has weakened you. Therefore, have patience for a little while, and I shall create for you helpers in pleading. Only follow my advice and let it be proclaimed to-day throughout the land that you decree to the Jews who dwell among your native people that they are forbidden to practise their beliefs and their customs until heaven grants you the son and heir of your glorious dominion.'

"Although the king did not grasp what all this had to do with the heir of his blood that he was to acquire, he assented to the proposal and had the announcement proclaimed in all of his lands. Then every Jewish heart was terrified. But since the Jews were devoted to their faith, they did not abandon it but served it with the same faithfulness as before during the dark nights and in secret cellars. Thus it came

about that the souls which during the day-time lay imprisoned in the claws of that malicious animal called anxiety,
sent upward in the night-time—when no one forbid them
their God—their united prayers that the Lord might grant
the king a child so that they might be liberated from their
servile shame. So fervent were they in their perseverance
that heaven was moved by the pressure of their prayers, and
the holy souls which live in the joy of God once again
trembled violently in response to the great earthly cry of
woe. But the spirit of the highest remained untouched. Then
one of the enlightened souls was so strongly seized by a
feeling of sympathy that it appeared before the throne of
the Eternal and requested, 'Let me return to earth, from
which you have raised me, so that I may be born to the king
as a son, to liberate the Jewish people.' This the Lord
granted.

"The son was born to the king. But in his happiness the
king forgot the Jews; he failed to end their oppression as
he had promised to, and there was no one in the land who
could act as a mediator for them.

"The child, however, was beautiful of face and charming
in his soul and inclined from his earliest years to thoughtful
seriousness and wisdom. It became evident later, when he
grew to be a youth, that the teachings of his tutor were
wasted on his clear spirit, in contrast with which they
seemed colourless and unsubstantial. The king did not know
whom to appoint as a mentor for his son. At that time, however, there was much talk in the royal city about an old
stranger who had come there for the first time a short while
ago and about whose origin there were indeed many con-

jectures but no sure information. Although the old man sought no one out and avoided market-place and street, much was related of his knowledge and of the power of his soul which caused people to turn to him as adviser and helper when the need arose. The people also spoke of the peculiar customs of his life and imagined him to be connected with higher powers.

"All this was told to the king, who sent for the mysterious man and requested of him that he dwell with him and educate the king's son. The wise man agreed on one condition. 'Command,' he said, 'that none enter into my study, either by force or by cunning, during the hours that I desire to spend alone!' This the king promised and charged all the household, including his own son, to heed the wish of the wise man.

"The king's son developed a strong love for the old man and became more attached to him than to his father. But he was pained by the fact that the teacher at times asked him to leave him, and after the manner of youth entreated the man with flattery and prayers that he might suffer him to remain during those secret moments, yet without ever receiving consent. Then he hid himself one day in a corner of the chamber behind a door which led to a balcony and waited with throbbing pulses. When the master had bolted the room and everything became still after a time, the king's son came out and found his teacher standing before a desk over an old book, clothed in a prayer shawl and his head crowned with phylacteries. The old man looked silently and anxiously in his face. Then the youth was woebegone. 'I did not want to grieve you in any way,' he cried, 'for I am faithful to you in the ground of my soul. Honour me with your confidence and tell me what your strange actions mean.'

"The old man related that he was by birth a Jew, that he was deprived of his faith through the command of the king and was condemned to secrecy. The youth was curious to learn something of the laws and nature of this faith, and the teacher gave him the knowledge he desired. Soon the king's son acquired an inclination for the holy Scriptures, and with great zeal the teacher now secretly instructed him day after day. The old, wonderful lives that arose out of the venerable letters overcame the boy, and he felt that he must openly choose and confess this new faith. He expressed this feeling to his teacher who counselled him that, if this were the case, he should throw off position and honour and flee with him to a strange land where they could live the teaching un-molested. This proposal pleased the youth.

"They came to a land where the Jewish people could practise their faith in peace and lived there in seclusion for many years. During this time the youth became great in knowledge. Then it happened that a zaddik came into the city and was received with honour by the Jews. The king's son and his teacher also hurried to greet him. The noble conduct of the youth pleased the zaddik so greatly that he offered him his only daughter in marriage. When the wedding ceremony was concluded, the king's son said to his young wife, 'I have a request to make of you this day. It happens at times, in moments of ecstasy, that my body lies as if lifeless and looks like that of a dead man. Do not then, I ask you, summon help to somehow animate me, but wait patiently for the time at which my soul will return of its own free will into the realm of bodily life.'

"The wife, who was of a sweet as well as courageous disposition, promised to heed this admonition well and did so in the future when circumstances required it. She was a gentle and happy companion to the man, and the two of them passed all of their time in loving communion. Then it happened that the husband fell into an unusually deep trance in which his body really appeared to be dead. The young wife at first bore the sight with steadfast courage, but then, when the usual span of time had elapsed, a bewildering anxiety overcame her. She wanted to summon aid but at once recalled the command and sank down silently beside the lifeless one.

"After long hours the first traces of returning life became evident in the body of the enraptured man. He arose and slowly came to his full senses. The wife wanted to greet him joyfully, but he responded to her words with melancholy, and it seemed to her as if his glance rested on her with a hidden sympathy. The whole day he remained absorbed and turned in·on himself. In the evening the wife entreated with loving urging that he not conceal from her what burdened his heart. 'Know, my wife,' he answered her, 'that a painful knowledge came to me to-day as I sojourned in the eternal heights. Because of my birth and because of the early years of my life, which I passed in pomp and idle worldliness in the court of the king, a higher ascent of the soul is barred to me unless I embrace death and then am reborn to a poor, pure, and humble woman. Therefore, I beg of you, my loved one and my spouse, that you remain of one spirit with me and do not stand in the way of my departing at once.'

" 'I am willing,' spoke the wife, 'if you will let me die with you and come back to earth with your soul and in your new youth be united to you once again as your wife.'

"They lay down together in the sleep of death and expired in the same breath. A space of time passed here below during which their souls were immersed in that darkness the duration of which one never measures, and then they returned. The man was born to a humble woman in the stillness of poverty, and the wife entered into the earthly light again in a humble cottage. Both their childhood and the years of their youth were spent in a long, unconscious seeking for the unknown which slept in the ground of the heart. They looked beyond life and those near them with strange eyes, each awaiting the consort of his soul. And you, friends, must all know that they have found each other and that they sit here among us, united as bride and bridegroom."

When the Baal-Shem ceased speaking, a splendour lay on all foreheads.

The Psalm-Singer

In a city not far from the city of the Baal-Shem lived a rich man who was disposed toward the service of God at the rare times of his self-communion, but usually gave himself up to the variegated impulses of the world. He had often heard of the saint and knew that all the pious visited him; yet he avoided him, whether because of shyness or because, laden with the burden of the everyday, he felt no urge toward the peace of the master. But the Baal-Shem knew about his life, as he knew about the life of all creatures, and loved him secretly from afar. For despite this man's thoughtlessness, an impulsive kindness dwelt in the ground of his noisy being. At times stifled by the desire for pleasure or eclipsed by suddenly raging anger, this kindness still broke forth powerfully ever again and afforded many poor and downtrodden people a modest sufficiency in the shadow of his expansive existence.

On one silent day of self-recollection, he found that he must do something for the glory of God and decided to have a Torah written. When the quiet had fled from his heart, he began the execution of his idea in his usual manner, with much ostentation and splendour. A famous Torah-writer was summoned. Then the rich man had the choicest animals slaughtered, distributed their flesh among the poor, and directed that the hides be worked to parchment and the holy books inscribed on them. The work took a long time and when completed was the wonder and talk of the city. The owner had a costly case made and a cover of fine material with ornaments of metal and stone. When everything stood there finished, he gave a feast for the city. Neither the poor nor the disfavoured were excluded, but all were welcomed to the meal.

For three days already his house had filled up every hour anew with men who sat at the long tables and ate and drank. His servants had had to fight off sleep for all these nights. Among them was one, an honest man, who was called the psalm-singer because the holy songs were never absent from his lips. He joined them to all the work that he did and recited them not like a book of the Scriptures but like the complaint of a man who suffers and knows God's ear to be at his mouth. The rich man often came quietly by and listened to him, and his heart sang with the singing. It seemed to him as if there lived in the song of the man the stillness which so seldom visited him, and in obedience to it he honoured him and never set him to hard work. During the days of the feast the psalm-singer, like the other servants, had waited on the tables incessantly and served the guests; yet the master of the house had assigned him to the visitors whom he valued most highly and whom he entertained in his own room.

Then it happened on the evening of the third day that the guests needed water for the blessing over the washing of the hands before mealtime. They called the servant, but he was nowhere to be found. Then the host himself went around the house to search for him and after awhile came upon him in one of the garrets, sleeping on a bed in his clothes. He called him, but the other was deep in sleep and gave no answer. Then rage arose in the master; he pulled the prone man up by the shoulders and shouted at him, "Go to the black year, you psalm-singer!"

The servant looked at the rich man with strange eyes. Then he said, "Sir, you imagine wrongly, if you believe that there is no one to uphold the rights of the poor psalm-singer." But the host paid no attention to his words and betook himself again to his guests.

As he went a little later from the main hall to the corridor of the house in order to greet a new-comer, a strange man entered the door, clothed like a servant. This man spoke to him and said, "Sir, my master has a matter to discuss with you that is of importance and that can brook no delay. Since something prevents him from coming to you, he asks if you will not mind the small trouble of climbing into the carriage which stands before your door. The way is short and the horses fast; you will lose very little time."

The rich man wondered over the strange servant and his peculiar affair, but something paralyzed his reflections, forbid him questions and forced him forward. In light house-

[*133*]

clothes he climbed into the carriage, and the vehicle moved rapidly away. The waxing moon moved upward in the heavens, huge as he had never before seen it. After awhile, which seemed to the man neither long nor short, he noticed that the hoof-beats of the horses became silent and the carriage nonetheless rushed onward. There was no longer any way, nor any left or right, no atmosphere above him and nothing of which his understanding was able to take possession. Everything in him was dissolved into an astonishment without expectation or fear. He felt that he had taken the step beyond, and what held before now held no longer.

Then the carriage halted. He followed a compulsion that was as incomprehensible as it was definite and climbed out. Glancing behind him, he perceived that the carriage, on whose step his foot had just rested, had disappeared. He stood in a lofty forest whose trees shot upward, slender and smooth, like towering columns. But he could not see the crowns, for they arched themselves too high and there was a milk-white fog between the trunks which robbed him of sight. Under his feet was crackling frost. It froze him with knifing pain in every limb. It forced him forward. He walked and walked, and it seemed to him as if faces emerged suddenly from the milky haze that took the place of the air, an undulating and moving of forms, no thicker than this fog itself and entirely blended with it. He wandered through all of this, and his going was without measure and comparison, as formerly his ride. Finally, there arose before him in the distance a light shining through the haze which guided him to a goal. The goal proved to be a house veiled by the fog, and the source of light was the door which stood open and let the clear radiance stream out.

He went up to it and entered. As soon as he had stepped over the threshold, the fog cleared to a crystalline air. He looked into a room whose ceiling was made out of sturdy rafters of an antique brown, but whose walls and floor were of a fresh and shining white. The room was filled with a sweet and comfortable warmth. Seven tall lights burned festively in a stand on the mighty table, emitting a strong fragrance. Against the walls stood chairs with lofty backs, old dark chairs, but spacious and commanding almost like thrones. Beyond this the visitor perceived nothing other than a huge, green, shimmering oven which filled a corner of the room. Anxious and as if imprisoned in a dream, he stepped nearer; he did not dare to touch table or chair, but rather hid himself behind the oven to await whoever should come. So he sat, and the glassy air sang strangely in his ears.

Then three men entered the room, one a short time after the other. They were ancient men, bowed and yet so tall that their heads seemed to touch the rafters of the ceiling. Ice-grey flowed their hair and beard, in whose waves it seemed as if time had interwoven itself. Behind the shadows of the white eye-lashes hid the sun and lightning of the eyes. The garments of the three were simple—linen and hide. They greeted one another by the names of the patriarchs with great, soft greetings, let themselves down into the chairs, and rested quietly as after long travels. While they sat, a fourth entered who was not so old and not so large, yet was clad in the garments and gestures of a ruler. He bowed respectfully as a grandson bows before his grandfather, and they greeted him with the name of David the King. Now he raised his voice, and the lights seemed about to shower sparks as he spoke. "I have a suit, O Fathers, against the man who sits behind the oven!" The words tore open the breast of the hidden man, and his own heart-beat rebelled against him. But the fathers raised their heads to listen.

"He who hides himself here," spoke the king, "has, with the curse of his mouth, cast the final horror on a defenceless retainer because of a trifle. Since this retainer is my servant and my song never dies on his lips, I have risen to his defence and demand here his right and that he who violated it be put to death for his offence."

To the rich man in his hiding-place it seemed as if the circulation of his blood had already ceased at the king's words. He raised his eyes that he might be afforded a final glance. Then he saw a man standing on the other side of the table and recognized him as one whom he had met at times during his life and whom the people had called the wonder-worker and the Master of the Name. The man stood exactly opposite the king, he bore his head high, and his eyes flashed. He caught up the king's last words while they still cut the air, raised his voice against him, and spoke, while the fathers, large and confident, looked across at him with silent turning of their heads. "Brother David, you come from heaven and yet you seem to me as if you still sat on your throne in Jerusalem! Do you wish to still a petty injury by means of an intolerable injury? Do you wish to blot out an evil with an evil? Do you wish to purify a weak revenge by a fiery revenge?"

"Do not trifle with me, brother!" the king answered him.
"I am not eager for revenge but for justice! Or is it your
opinion that the faithful retainer should be trampled under
foot while his tormentor persists proud and unpunished?"

But the voice of the Baal-Shem raised itself like an arch-
angel's voice forged in eternity. "Brother and King," he
spoke, "a stranger is my guest, and the young shepherd has
a rosy face and shining eyes, and nonetheless band and
crown weigh on his forehead, which is without shadow—
King," said the Baal-Shem, "a king's soul is in me. It came
to me as I returned to life this latest time through the body
of a woman. In the hours of the night, it talks to me, pressed
close to the root of my ear. Although it is very shy, it is
quite intimate with me. And it speaks out of the primal
depths: 'I stood with him when he said to his faithful subject, "Go down to your house," and I heard when he said
to him on another day, "Why have you not gone down to
your house?" and was with him on the day, which came
after this, when he wrote the letter, "Place him facing the
heaviest battle and withdraw from him so that he may be
struck down and die!" Then I removed myself from him
with blood and pain and have been wounded and sore from
that hour on!' "

Then David lifted his forehead under the golden ring,
forehead and crown gleaming, and as he spoke a deep stream
flowed under his voice, "I have been too deeply submerged
in the most terrible revenge and have climbed to the light,
the seam of my mantle was black and stuck with blood
which had been shed, and I have borne my song upward
with me. For my song was born to me out of sin and stain,

do not judge

[137]

and it awakened in me a new soul and ascended, and there was peace between God and me."

After these words of the king, the countenance of the Baal-Shem was transformed. Mysteries and revelations glided over it, and beholding it was like beholding the firmament when it gradually unveils its landscape and the shining plain opens up behind the clouds. Then the Baal-Shem spoke, and his voice was transformed, "Your song is the diamond bridge which leads upward out of the valley of depravity to the heart of God. If in one night it groans aloud out of the breast of a monster, it is, nonetheless, an angel which bears him above the spheres and puts him to sleep in the lap of God. When your song took me by the hand, I forgot justice, and when it smiled at me, all opposition disappeared from within me."

Then the king bowed his head before the master, and out of the timeless there rushed upward a great movement as when a mystery fulfils itself and then sinks down.

A white beam of light passed over the eyes of the man behind the oven. He stood in his house and held the latch of the door of his chamber. There were the guests, washing their hands for the evening meal.

The Disturbed Sabbath

This week, as on every other week, the Baal-Shem drove out of the city at the termination of the Sabbath, and with him were the three disciples who were called the three Davids—namely, Rabbi David of Mikolayev, Rabbi David Firkes, and Rabbi David Leikes—and the servant Aleksa who directed the horses. Ordinarily, the master determined the direction and speed of the journey by means of his will and without any speech; the servant Aleksa could turn his back on the horses, yet they brought the carriage to the desired place at the desired time. But this time the Baal-Shem felt that his will was powerless in the face of the strong tug of the horses, and he saw how the carriage conveyed them to an unknown goal and accepted no command from the frightened coachman. Then he wanted to turn around, called aloud, and seized hold of the reins himself; but he had no power over the horses. Contrary to the bid-

ding of his hand, they ran on at a fast trot to where the
invisible force was driving them. Thus they came to a
wilderness into which they drew the carriage until there
was neither path nor open view, and they roamed around
in the wilderness with cramped, regular steps.

This lasted three days, and the Baal-Shem bore it as a divine
ordinance against which no human soul might dare murmur;
but the disciples sat there stunned and miserable, and the
servant Aleksa acted like one gone mad, as if he had never
before experienced anything out of the ordinary with his
master. After the third day, however, a new urge came over
the horses; they ran out of the wilderness into an adjoining
forest and hauled the carriage into the deep thicket. There
they remained standing and neighed comfortably as if they
had returned to their stall and had the finest fodder before
them.

But those in the carriage could no longer distinguish between day and night. They nourished themselves scantily
from the few provisions which they had brought with
them, and no sleep came over them, so overpoweringly did
anxiety grip their hearts. Hours passed and still more hours.
But one came in which the Baal-Shem recognized by the
sevenfold sadness which pressed on his spirit that the day
before the Sabbath had arrived, and he did not know how
he and his disciples would be able to receive and honour
the holy day. In his deep need he felt a comfortless weariness come over his limbs and fell finally into a dull sleep.

Now a hope came into the souls of the disciples, for they
knew how that which seemed dark and confused when he
was awake became clear when he lay sleeping with his

senses closed off. Yet the Baal-Shem awoke in a restless mood, and the stiffness which lay on him had grown almost to a lameness. But then he lifted himself up, raised his arm, and pointed with trembling finger into the distance. A gleam of light was visible behind the thick briars. So they left the carriage and progressed with great difficulty in the direction of the growing light. Soon the sun stood over their heads and they recited "Blessed be the Lord and blessed be His name!" In the distance they saw a small house that lay like a dull, grey patch in the midst of the forest clearing.

They went up to the house. Before the door stood a gigantic, bull-necked man with red-gold, bristly hair and uncouth, naked feet. This man was clothed in the manner of those frivolous people who disdain the good customs of the fathers. Moreover, the prescribed fringes were nowhere to be seen on his clothes. He pressed his fists against his sides, stared scornfully at the approaching men, and remained silent. They bowed to him and asked, "Would it be possible for us to celebrate the holy Sabbath in your house?"

Then he bellowed at them, "I do not want you and will not suffer you to cross my threshold! Do I not know you? Your faces betray you. You are Hasidim who drag your piety to the market-place and preach on the streets. Go, I am proof against your idle words. I hate you, I hate all of you from yesterday and from all time past and forever. My father hated you and my grandfather before him; you are odious to my house. Therefore, go from here quickly, for I do not want to see your faces any longer."

But they bore his words in silence and asked only, "Then

tell us whether there are other dwellings near by to which we could go in order to celebrate the holy Sabbath."

The man laughed fiercely and roared, "As much time as it took you to get here, so much time and more will you need until you come to another human place!"

When he had said this and then laughed again and again in the same manner, as if he would never stop, their new-found courage threatened to desert them again. But Rabbi David Firkes, the youngest of the Davids, who usually never said a word, but was, instead, in the habit of sitting silent in the company of disciples, stepped forward and spoke to the man softly and peaceably, "It may be that this and that tells against us in your mind. But is it really true that you wish to thrust us out into the wilderness? Consider, the Sabbath is your and our sanctuary, and when we walk about in it, we must somewhere and sometime meet your steps too. Do you wish to ruin the Sabbath of the future? Behold, the Lord is your and our God, and if you will master your rage, you will perceive how he looks at you."

Then the man was silent and looked from one to the other without speaking. But Rabbi David of Mikolayev, the oldest of the Davids, who considered himself well-versed in the impulses of the human heart and in the nature of hidden human motives, said, "Consider also that we do not ask any present of you. Rather we want to pay you as much as you may demand, even though it be ten times what is customary in most places."

The man looked away from him contemptuously, turned to the youngest and said in a brusque tone, "So be it. But do not think that you can bring your Sabbath into my

house. Here my custom and my law alone prevail. Therefore, give heed to what I command you. In the first place,
I know well that you spend much time in preparing yourself for prayer, that you pay no attention to how late in the
day it is, but wait until grace takes hold of you. But here
this sitting and gazing does not go. I shall pray what there is
to pray and then proceed to eat, for I need much food and
must satisfy my hunger often and quickly. In the second
place, I know your manner of praying, how you walk and
rave, and each one wants to speak to God louder than the
other. But there is no room here for the uproar of your
ecstasies, and I shall not let myself be bothered by you. In
third place, you love to criticize the meal and, like proper
fools, to weigh for a long time whether this or that is pure
enough for you Hasidim. That too will not be allowed
here."

Such misunderstanding and misrepresentation of their
holy customs and the prohibition against practising them
was hard for the Baal-Shem and his followers; but there was
no way open to them but this, and so they promised to obey
in all respects. Then he bade them enter. They came into a
narrow and barren little room. When they had stretched
themselves out on the floor for awhile and had recovered
from the worst of their fatigue, the Baal-Shem asked
whether there was a stream or reservoir in the neighbourhood where they could take an immersion-bath in honour of
the Sabbath. At this the man again fell into a rage and cried,
"I did in fact suspect something of the sort. You are a miserable pack of thieves! You only want to spy around in
order to discover where I keep my goods. I shall take your

odds and ends and throw them out and you with them!"
Then they had to plead for a long time and seek reconcilia-
tion until he again showed himself inclined to let them stay.

Now the Baal-Shem and his followers sat there, looked at
the man, who went up and down in the room, and marvelled
at him; for they had never before seen a man so coarse,
crude, and unclean as this one. In the room too the walls and
floor were besmirched, and neither table nor bench stood
there, but four stakes were driven into the floor, and on
them lay a rude plank. Soon they noticed that this was the
only room that was lived in; there were indeed other rooms
in the house, but they were all locked up and the doors
were grey with dust as if they were never opened. What is
more, a living house-companion was nowhere to be seen,
not even a cat or a bird.

Evening was near, and still they could espy neither
utensils nor food in honour of the Sabbath. The giant man
wandered about idly, at times cut himself a slice of an enormous water-melon which lay in the corner and stuck it in
his mouth, then again hummed to himself in the manner of
peasants. The companions were overcome by the fear that
he would not be able to observe the Sabbath at all and that
he would deny it the consecration that Jews all over the
world perform with zeal. But then he took a piece of crude,
unbleached linen cloth and spread it out on his miserable
table. On it he laid a small heap of clay, bored a hole with
his finger and set a wretched wax candle in it. Now he began
to recite the lovely words with which since ancient times,
week after week in all lands of the earth, the Sabbath has
been received as the bride of our souls. But he spoke them

as do the fools who swallow the sounds and stifle the sense
of the words. In an instant he had finished the prayer, and
the guests had to do the same, bound by their promise. As
much as his nature pained them, they could not nourish any
hatred against him in the face of the holiness of the evening
and called out to him, "Good Sabbath!"

But he snorted at them by way of answer, "May a bad
year come to you!"

When they wanted to strike up the song, "Peace be with
you!" he flew out at them and made them keep still. Then
he prepared to speak the blessing over the wine. They
begged him to give them some wine in order that they
themselves might make the blessing, but he refused them
and cried out, "If you were all to say the blessing, the light
would soon be gone. Let me alone do it for you." And so he
took the goblet between two fingers and muttered the
words to himself. Then he opened his mouth wide and
poured the wine inside, so that only a few drops remained
at the bottom of the goblet. He handed it to them and
said, "There, you drunkards, but don't drink too much or
you will get tipsy."

Now he laid on the table a hard, mouldy bread made out
of black meal and rye and broke off a piece for everybody.
When one of the disciples wanted to reach for the loaf in
order to cut off a second slice, the host thrust him back and
said to his guests, "Do not dare to touch my bread with
your disgusting hands." Then he set before them a tureen
with thin lentil broth, laid before each a huge spoon and
bid them reach in and eat, since here there were no soup
bowls or other such refinements. As he said this, he leaned

over the tureen, scooped out a spoonful of broth, and ate with such greedy haste that the soup fell out of the corners of his mouth and flowed back into the tureen. The companions could no longer bring themselves to stretch out a hand for the food. After the meal they wanted to sing the Sabbath songs, but this too he forbade them. He reeled off mechanically the table prayer, neglecting all the traditional customs, and got up to prepare for his guests a mean couch on the floor.

In the early morning they awoke and heard their host walking about singing, as if it were a peasant dance, the morning song that begins with the words, "The souls of all living." In that way he began the day, and it was still more painful than the evening had been. The Baal-Shem had lost all power of inner vision, the holy wisdom had forsaken him, and so he sat, clasped his hands, and could think of nothing other than "Why and what is this that God has done to me here?" Finally night arrived and sleep came gently and kindly over him. When he arose in the morning, he felt a new strength springing up in him, and he prayed with all his might, for he never journeyed from a place without having talked with God. Then he ordered the servant Aleksa to take out the horses, which had been brought into the stall, and hitch them to the wagon. But the servant returned immediately and reported that the house door was locked. Then the master went to the host, asked him to open the door, and added, "Take our thanks for all the friendship which you have shown us and show us now the way whereby we can return to our home most quickly."

"By no means," the latter answered. "Rather you will still

remain my guests." He would not let himself be prevailed upon and held them in his house until the fourth day, virtual prisoners.

On the morning of the fourth day he came to them and said, "Today I shall open the door for you." While he said this, he looked at them in a strange way and left. Then a horror came over the disciples, for they did not understand his expression, and the thought crept into their minds that he might want to murder them.

But while they gave way to such fear, the door of one of the closed-off rooms opened, and a beautiful and finely clothed woman stepped forth and bowed before the master. "Rabbi," she said, "I beg of you that you and your disciples might celebrate the holy Sabbath with me."

"You call me Rabbi," the Baal-Shem replied. "How then could you allow my Sabbath to be disturbed in this way?"

Then the woman asked, "Rabbi, do you not recognize me?"

"No, I do not recognize you," he answered.

"When I was still almost a child," she related, "I served in your house. I was an orphan and had no one in the world. But my hands were cursed with such awkwardness that many costly vessels that I carried I let fall to the ground and shatter. Your wife frequently reproved me for this. Once the Sabbath table was ready and your wife wished to bring in the tureen. But I wanted to show that I had become more dexterous and asked that the Sabbath tureen be placed in my hands. No sooner did I hold it, however, than a trembling came over my fingers, and I let the tureen fall. Your wife grew angry with me and gave me a light blow in the face. But you sat near by, saw it, and let it take place without saying a word.

"Then a judgement was pronounced on you in heaven: because of your silence, you should lose your share in the world to come. But later the grace was accorded to me to be wed by this man, who is a hidden zaddik who conceals his holiness behind his conduct. It was he who disclosed to me what had been ordained for you. Then we began to pray to God that the judgement be changed, our prayer was granted us, and the judgement became milder and ever milder until it was pronounced that one of your Sabbaths must be disturbed, for the Sabbath is, in fact, the source of the world to come. And we were assigned to do this to you. But only if it were accomplished in every detail, so we were told, would our deed remove the judgement from you. So, with aching hearts, we have done it. And now your portion is at the head of the highest paradise."

At this moment wisdom returned to the master, his inner vision was restored, he saw into the depths of destiny and saw the holy and mysterious man stand before him as he really was. So they went together into the ornamented rooms, remained with each other this day and the next, and celebrated the Sabbath with great joy.

The Conversion

Among the most zealous of those who opposed the Baal-
Shem was Rabbi Jacob Joseph of Sharigrod. In no one else,
perhaps, did the opposing will stream from so deep a source.
For the heretical things which infuriated him lay like presentiment and seed in his own soul, completely hidden beneath the realm of words, indeed entirely underneath that
chamber of the mind in which thought is born.

But there were three customs of the new sect which,
above all, evoked the enmity of the rabbi: the joy of their
feasts, which broke down the fence around the holy law
and foamed up in dance and song; the irregularity of their
service, for the community only loosely embraced the
praying men and, in fact, each spoke to God for himself
and in his own way, often too with wild gestures; but more
than all, the gentle sermon, vibrating with mystery, which
the master preached after the third Sabbath meal. The rabbi

had often heard of this sermon. It was not built on the interpretation of the Scriptures, as custom ordained—a foundation upon which, ordinarily, interpretation ingeniously towered on interpretation. It spoke of the things of the soul, as if one had the right to talk about them. Often it was an altogether ordinary anecdote, such as the common folk tell one another in tap-rooms; but it was spoken slowly and solemnly as if it were the mystery of the *kedusha*, and the people listened to it as if it continued the revelation on Sinai. As often as the rabbi was told of this, he was again overpowered by anger as on the first time. Anecdotes on the Sabbath! What sort of meaning could anecdotes have? And still more indignant than before, he ordered the voice to keep still which awakened in him far below and which pretended to know that meaning. He exhorted his soul to follow the true path of perfection through turning away from the living, through discipline and mortification.

Once the Baal-Shem got ready in the evening and drove to Sharigrod. He was without companions and conversed with the summer night as with a friend. As the night took leave and the day was still slowly rising, the carriage came into the small city. There lay the houses in the dawn light with closed window-shutters, like joyless slumberers with heavy lids. Compassion welled up in the Baal-Shem for all those who pursued their dull morning sleep behind these windows. He walked up and down with steady strides in the growing light of day until after awhile a man came along the way, driving before him several animals which he pastured during the day on the meadow before the town. To him the master began to speak and, since the man at first answered him briefly and shyly, he gradually fell into narrating a story.

As the Baal-Shem talked a second man came up, soon after a third, then ever more and more, mostly servants and poor people who begin the day early. They all remained standing, listened eagerly and called over still others from the houses. As the hour advanced, the maids came with their water-jugs on the way to the fountain and stopped, the children came running out of the rooms, and the family heads themselves left their businesses and their pursuits to hear the strange man. His narration, however, was so delightfully intertwined that whenever some one came up it seemed to that person to be at the beginning, and those who earlier had not been curious were now entirely concentrated on what would happen next and awaited it as if it were the fulfilment of their most precious hopes. Thus they all had one great story, and within it each had his own small and all-important story. The small stories intercrossed and clasped one another, but in an instant they were again disentangled and in order and ran along parallel to one another, very neat and proper. If one departed, then it left behind a new promise which soon prepared to lead forth a comrade.

After a little the whole town was in the market-place, all were listening, and each had forgotten what otherwise he was obliged to do at this hour. The workmen held their tools in their hands and the housewives their ladles. At the very front, however, stood the synagogue servant, carrying a great ring of keys with which he was just on his way to open the synagogue. The story had taken such possession

of him that he had pressed through the crowd to right before the master and now stood and listened with his ears
and his heart and his whole body, as little mindful of his
duties as of a forgotten dream.

But the narration of the Baal-Shem was not like your nar-
rations, children of the present, which are twisted like a little
human destiny or round like a little human thought. Rather
the vari-coloured magic of the sea was in them and the white
magic of the stars and, most ineffable of all, the soft wonder
of the infinite air. And yet it was no report of distant times
and places that the story told; rather, under the touch of its
words, the secret melody of each person was awakened, the
ruined melody which had been presumed dead, and each
received the message of his dispersed life, that it was still
there and was anxious for him. It spoke to each, to him
alone, there was no other; he was everyone, he was the tale.

Then the master raised his glance. Smiling, he looked
into the distance, saw, through houses and walls, how the
rabbi stood before the door of the prayer house, come to
perform his prayer at this hour. The house was locked and
the servant missing, and they all were missing who gathered
day after day at this time and awaited him. The Baal-Shem
looked into the spirit of the rabbi; he saw how rage and
bitterness grew in him and how he mastered his vexation
and forced himself to be patient. Then the master decided
to release the servant from the story. The unbinding came
over the man suddenly, like an awakening, and without stopping to reflect, he ran as fast as he could to the prayer-
house.

When he reached the door, he found the rabbi, with

knitted brow, his eyes cast down to the ground. The rabbi repressed the words of displeasure and merely demanded, with a brusque movement, that he open quickly. But the servant, still filled by and immersed in the story, was aware neither of his own negligence nor of his master's annoyance. Instead he began to tell about the strange man who was standing on the square and narrating stories with all the people gathered around him. He described the figure and appearance of the stranger, and then the rabbi knew who had come and who it was who was striving with him over the souls, and a wrathful light came into his eyes. Without a word he shoved the servant aside, entered the house and began to pray.

After awhile it happened that a man from among the pious of the Baal-Shem and from his city betrothed his daughter to one of the favourite pupils of the rabbi of Sharigrod. The wedding was to take place in the city of the Baal-Shem.

Rabbi Jacob Joseph was deeply distressed by this betrothal. When he learned of it, it affected him as if his son had fallen among bad companions. Love, to be sure, proved stronger than anger when the pupil himself appeared before him and told him all about it, and he was forced to give the match his blessing. But he refused the entreaty of the pupil to come to the great celebration in Mesbitz and explained that he could not now or ever enter the abode of the heretic. Nonetheless, the youth pressed him day after day with urgent beseeching until finally the words escaped the rabbi, "How can I go with you? As soon as you and your friends will go to any place in Mesbitz, it will be to the unholy man who is destroying the people of Israel!" Then the pupil, in order to win a favourable reply from his teacher, promised that he would not look on the countenance of the Baal-Shem, and on this condition the rabbi consented to travel with him.

When they were under way, however, and were stopping at an inn not far from their destination, he noticed his pupil conversing secretly with his friends, and he realized that they must be speaking about how to contrive to enter the house of the Baal-Shem without the knowledge of the rabbi. Then he went up to them and said to the bridegroom, "I have done wrong to impose upon you a condition which you cannot fulfil. Since I do not want to set out alone on the journey home, I shall remain here until you travel homeward from the wedding and then return with you to my city." The pupil stammered out new entreaties and promises, but the rabbi paid no heed to him and instead turned to the host and bade him show him to a room where he could pursue his studies.

A little later he sat in his silent room with his book lying open before him. But when he leaned over it and wished to begin to read, he was startled by the behaviour of the letters. Instead of docilely standing there in their fine structure, as always before—each joyfully awaiting for him to come to it, proudly content when he had read it—they swung in a mad dance and threw their limbs in the air. Indeed, a thick, round letter turned head over heels continuously without tiring. The rabbi closed his eyes, opened them again, and as the letters showed no signs of putting an end to their scandalous conduct, he brought his hand down violently on the book. Then in an instant all the letters were silent and well-behaved, each sat in its place as if it had never moved from there, and a pair of letters in the forefront even had ready the attitude of joyful expectation. But when the rabbi now wished to begin to read, there pressed toward him from out of the book a confused medley of a hundred small voices. These were the words which struggled with one another. There were not two camps of fighters; rather each word opposed all the others, and each affirmed that it was surrounded by liars and hypocrites, whose object was simply to rob him of his native rights and who behaved this way out of malicious envy since they had neither meaning nor soul of their own. And when the rabbi had also composed this brawl, the sentences arose and declared that they were no longer willing to serve an unknown end that floated over them all but intended instead to live from and for themselves.

The rabbi looked at the book and smiled. Then he closed it and smiled again. He still had a book in his mind, a great and superabundant one that no one could derange. But when he tried to summon the first thought, his smile broke off. For no thought arose; there was only a dull forgetting that spread out as over a neglected graveyard. Then the rabbi was terrified, and this terror overwhelmed him like a great peril of death. Now he understood that he was commanded to go to Mesbitz. Forthwith his thoughts revived in him, so precipitously, in fact, that he was almost terrified for a second time.

It did not enter his mind to hire a wagon; he stepped out of the house and walked. When he came to Mesbitz, he was borne along farther, without questioning his eyes or his will, until he found himself before a great house standing apart, from which the light of many candles and the speech of many voices pressed toward him. He knew that this was the house of the Baal-Shem. Suddenly all was still. It seemed to the rabbi as if the light grew three times brighter, and out of the silence a voice began to speak which resounded so wonderfully that he had to draw nearer and listen. And he heard what the voice spoke:

"I shall tell you a story.

"There was once a rabbi, a wise and severe man. He sat in his chamber on the night of the Ninth of Ab and mourned for the Temple and for Jerusalem. And this year his grief was different from what it had been in all past years on this night. For in other years he had felt as though he had been set down amid the destruction of the city and beheld with his own eyes the burning and the ravaging. But on this night he felt as though he were a pillar in the house of the Lord, and he felt on him the hand of the Chaldean who shattered it, and again he felt as if he were the metal of a broken pillar which was carried to Babylon. And the lament came out of his mouth not as out of one who saw and grieved, but as the groaning of a shattered pillar. And, not as one who comes and goes, but as a thing that has lived in glory and now is dashed to pieces and dragged into the final disgrace, he cried out to Jerusalem, 'Arise, shout in the night at the beginning of the watch, pour out your heart before the Lord like water!' And he came to feel that he was Jerusalem the city, the burning and the ravaging swept over him, and the thousandfold devastation happened to his limbs. A shriek broke out of him; it shook him like one dying and threw him on his bed.

"As he lay there, his body was poor in life like the body of one who lies dying. The hours of night moved along and spread over the prostrate man, destitute of all sensation, as if time had turned to sand and trickled down on him to bury him. About midnight, however, he felt a movement in the air, and a breeze touched his forehead, a living breath. He opened his eyes and became aware of the figure of a boy leaning over him, and he recognized the face of one of his pupils, whose delicate features were now distorted by fright. The boy touched his hand and spoke with trembling voice, 'Rabbi, you lie like one whose soul is poised for flight, ready to abandon him. You must take a little food in order to strengthen your life.'

"The rabbi turned his head and whispered and his teeth knocked against one another, 'Child, what are you saying? To-day is still the Ninth of Ab, a day of mourning and of fasting!'

"But the child clasped his hand tighter in his two warm hands and begged, 'Rabbi, remember that it is forbidden to place oneself voluntarily in the hands of death!' He left and returned carrying a large bowl of splendid fruit which he clasped in his arms. He knelt down before the rabbi, looked at him imploringly and imploringly bowed his head.

"And the rabbi, enlivened by the gay colours and the pleasant smells, sat upright and spoke the blessing over the fruit of the tree as one does who is preparing to eat. But as the last word escaped his lips, he was suddenly seized by horror at his deed. He raised his hand against his pupil and shouted at him, 'Take yourself off, tempting spirit who borrows a familiar form in order to delude me!' The boy took flight.

"But the rabbi fell into a deep sadness. Before him appeared the years of his life with all their sacrifice and self-denial, with the great control over himself which grew from year to year. And then there appeared before him a small wish with lustreless eyes which dragged itself up to the years like a sick dwarf and wiped them away with its finger so that nothing of them was left.

"Ever deeper became the sadness of the rabbi until the mourning of the day and the suffering over Jerusalem were submerged in this sadness. The sadness swallowed them and spread itself over his soul with scourge and firebrand. Now there was no longer in the rabbi anything of the hour when he had been a pillar in the house of the Lord and when he had been the city under the hand of the disaster, but rather he was this man, lying here on a bed in the night, this man who had hoarded and hoarded, with stern and never-tiring hand, and whom now a sick dwarf had robbed of everything with the sudden movement of a lean finger in the darkness. Above and around him he felt the night, stagnating and unchangeable.

"The night did not stagnate, however, but flowed over him. Before it disappeared, it laid its hand on his eyes and bestowed on him sleep. But from somewhere a seed fell into his sleep, and a dream sprouted and grew.

"The dream led the rabbi under the open midday sky which looked down on him through the tree-tops of a large fruit-garden. He walked through the narrow winding paths of the garden, bordered by high grass and by drooping branches heavily laden with fruit. Thus he came to the end of the garden and looked out over the low wall, and what he saw was the narrow lanes of the city in which he lived. But he knew well in his dream that there was no garden of this sort in his dwelling-place. Wondering fearfully, he went back and looked for some one who could give him information. As he approached the middle of the garden, where all the paths ran together and crossed, he saw a man in the clothes of a gardener. He was stooped to the earth, but he raised his forehead toward him now and looked at him with flashing eyes. 'Whose is this garden?' the rabbi asked him.

"The man replied, 'It belongs to the rabbi of this city.'

" 'I am the rabbi of this city,' responded the rabbi in astonishment. 'I am poor and have no property. How did this garden come to me?'

"Then lightning shot out of the man's eyes, and thunder rolled in his voice. 'Out of the pain of a wish, out of guilt and shame, out of a vain blessing, the hell of this garden was born to you.' He stamped with his foot, then the earth split open to its fiery core and the rabbi saw the intertwined roots of the trees descend into the primal depths where, united with one another, they nourished themselves on the flames.

"Then he awoke. The terror of the dream oppressed him until the evening when the day of mourning ended. Now the rabbi lifted himself, tore himself out of the embrace of the dream, and locked the door. He took the book of Psalms in his hand, stood and spoke the Psalms in a powerful voice. When he had spoken the first book, a cry came out of the distance from the night outside, 'Enough, the fruits have already fallen off!' But the rabbi raised his head and his voice and spoke the second book. When he had finished, the cry came again, and it sounded nearer and more distinct, 'Enough, the leaves have already withered!' Still the rabbi renewed his strength and prayed the third book. Now the voice was quite near, the windows rattled from its breath, and it called out, 'Enough, the twigs have already dried up!' The rabbi strained all the power of his soul and read the fourth book. Then the floor of his house shook, and the voice resounded as if it came from out of the earth beneath his feet, 'Enough, the boughs have already wasted away!' The rabbi felt now exhaustion was stealing over him, but he tore the innermost strength out of himself and the last book arose from his mouth and ascended like the smoke of a sacrifice. When he became silent, the locked door of the chamber sprang wide open, in it stood a dark messenger, panting as after a wild race and screaming, 'Enough, enough, you have conquered us, the trunks have already burst.' The figure faded away with its last word.

"Thus it happened at that time. Days, months, and years have passed by since then. But the roots of the garden have remained in the earth, and during many a night the rabbi ponders in vain how he might uproot them."

Thus the voice within narrated in the bright hall. Rabbi Jacob Joseph stood in the shadow, his forehead pressed to the wall, and the words fell into his heart. When the voice within grew silent, he plunged through the door into the hall and unto the feet of the Baal-Shem and cried, "Master, teach me what I must do to tear out the roots!"

"Know that this garden was not born to you out of your wish," spoke the Baal-Shem, "but out of that wish's pain because you supposed yourself defiled, suffered over yourself, and scattered affliction over your head like ashes. You thereby gave the light image of your wish a firm existence and sank its roots into the realm of the corporeal, whereas before it was only a shadow. But as I have told you this, the body of your wish has become a word and a hovering breath and lighter than the lightest image of your wish had been. And because I, a joyful man, have told your story to joyful men, joy has entered the depths and has torn out the roots."

Rabbi Jacob Joseph afterwards became the great disciple who preserved the teaching of the master in writing and handed it down to the generations to come.

The Return

On the anniversary of the death of the Rabbi of Ropshitz many zaddikim had gathered in Ropshitz. They were sitting there together in sadness when the door flew open and a woman with flashing eyes rushed in, threw herself on the floor, and cried, "Be merciful to me, you masters, and hear what a cruel misfortune has befallen me! Just a few weeks ago I had handed over to a Jew eight hundred silver gulden with which to travel to the villages to buy flax. It was a sure profit and we were going to share it half and half. Several days went by after that without my hearing anything from him, and I became uneasy in my heart. Just to-day, early in the morning, there came into my house a man who is native to this region, and I learned from him that my partner had met a sudden death, and neither money nor bills of sale were found on him. Now I ask and I demand what has happened to my money? Rabbis, tell me how to get it back!

You sit here together in glory like the archangels of the Lord, heaven stands over your head like an open gate!"

The distress of the woman touched the souls of some of the zaddikim, and they said, "Hold your peace, we shall do what is necessary to recover your money."

But now the zaddik Rabbi Shalom of Kaminka stood up and cried out, "Listen, all of you, and you too, woman! No promise can bind here. The money must remain lost for all time. Who is able to seize hold of the chain that runs over the wheel of all the ages! It must be that you brought an unpaid debt with you from a past life; this Jew was born in order to make good your debt, and since he has done that he has departed. You, however, should be thankful that the default of your soul is cancelled out!"

When he had said this, Rabbi Shalom turned to the zaddikim and said, "My teachers, if it pleases you, listen to me and I shall tell you a story of the holy Baal-Shem whose merit strengthens us.

"There lived in Risha in the days of the holy man a distinguished Jew, a rich man, well-versed in the Scriptures. Although he did not count himself among the Hasidim, he received with eager curiosity the reports of the astonishing deeds that the master had performed. Thus there grew in him the longing to see him in person. One day he had his travelling carriage made ready, ordered the coachman and the servants to mount, and drove as grandly as a nobleman to Mesbitz, the dwelling-place of the Baal-Shem. He fully intended when he entered the Baal-Shem's house to let the latter perceive his learning, for he hoped that he might thus be deemed worthy to discuss the interpretation of the

[*163*]

Bible with him or the mysteries of the Kabbala. But the Baal-Shem avoided anything of the sort and spoke simply and meditatively of all kinds of worldly matters. It seemed to the rich man that the Baal-Shem showed him no special honour by his speech. Still he wished to take leave in a worthy way, and so he silently laid a package of rubles before him on the table. The Baal-Shem saw this, a light smile slipped over his face, and it was as if he mused on a past event.

" 'But now, friend,' he then said, 'you must tell me what you lack and for what purpose I can intercede for you.'

"Thereupon the rich man replied, and in his words he placed a proud satisfaction, 'To me there is wanting—may God's Name be blessed—nothing. My house has its comfort, my children have grown up to the joy of my soul, my daughters have brought me respected sons-in-law, grandchildren are growing up in my house. . . . No, Master, I lack nothing!'

" 'Well,' thought the Baal-Shem, 'such a gift is a rare thing and not to be taken amiss.' It had hardly ever befallen him that some one had come before him and offered him a gift without at the same time tearing open his heart and pouring out the acid of his sufferings. The one asked him to look at a terribly painful wound for which he sought a cure, another wept that his unfruitful wife might bear him children, a third was threatened by prison and wanted to escape it. But here was a man who gave only and desired nothing.

" 'Why then have you come to me?' he asked.

" 'I only wanted to see you,' the man replied, 'for your wonder lives in the people and you are called a holy man.

But I said to my soul, I shall go there and come to know him by face and by voice.'

"To this the Baal-Shem responded, 'Now, friend, if it is true that you have made this long journey merely in order to stand before me with eye and ear, then look at me well and listen to me—I shall tell you a story to take with you on your way. But, friend, listen carefully to me! My story took place in this way:

" 'Once there dwelt in a city two rich Jews, neighbours, each of whom had a son. The youths were of the same age, they invented games for each other, learned together and loved each other with unswerving love. But how short are the days of unburdened youth! They both grew up and were early given in marriage by their parents. The one moved many miles away toward the south, the other still farther in the other direction.

" 'But now, friend, listen carefully to me. The two young people were at home in their love for each other, the world was still strange to them, and so they wrote long letters to each other every week, and these letters were their life. Gradually, however, their glance clung to what immediately surrounded and concerned them, and that sucked itself fast to their minds. Despite this they wrote every month and did not conceal from each other what befell them. But then the world clasped them in its arms and crushed the free breath out of their souls, and they were ashamed to confess to each other in letters that that stillness out of which the living word of love comes had withdrawn from their hearts. So finally they remained silent altogether, and only the reports from strange mouths spun threads between them now and then. Each heard of the other that he was housed in comfort and was of importance in his world.

" 'After many years it happened that one of them lost all that which had made him joyful and secure, indeed, he could no longer even call a respectable garment his own.

" 'As he now stood in this condition and struggled against misery, he thought of the friend of his youth and said to himself, "He who was once the whole world to me and much more beautiful than the world itself might ever become later on, he will restore me from out of this need if I only go to him." He borrowed the money for the journey under humiliating circumstances, rode to the city in which his friend lived, and visited him. There he was received with warmth of heart, and the whole house joined in a feast. As they sat side by side at the meal, the friend asked, "You soul of my childhood, tell me, how does it fare with you in the world?" "I cannot say much," the other replied. "Know simply that the very clothes that I wear are not mine." And as he talked, tears of pain flowed from his eyes and fell on the fine linen which covered the dining-table. Then his comrade asked no more, and the meal continued with jest, song, and game.

" 'When the meal was over and the friends sat side by side, the master of the house called his clerk and bid him draw up a statement of his entire fortune and when that was done to divide it all into equal halves and to give one of them to the brother of his heart.

" 'The poor man of a few days before rode home richly blessed, soon experienced the union of work and success, and in a few years his house was richer than it had ever been before. During the same period of time, however, it happened that misfortune was a guest at the house of the other friend, and he proved to be a stiff-necked fellow who would not give way even when the man used all his powers to dislodge him. Nor did the man meet along his bitter way any heart who would give him advice and assistance.

" 'As want, like a great thirsty spider, now wove him into its grey web and he breathlessly felt it become ever closer and tighter, he happened to think of the friend of his childhood. He wrote to him immediately and without hesitation since he had learned that his wealth had grown far beyond his former possessions. He proposed to come to him in his great affliction in order, without shame, to ask help from his hand. And he let him know on what day and at what hour he would leave the city in order to take the way to him. Then, at the right time, already full of joy, he set out on foot on the long journey. He hardly noticed the great weariness which finally overtook him; behind every bend of the road, in every distant cloud of dust, he hoped to catch sight of the coach of his frend coming to meet him since his friend knew the day when he had set out on his trip. Already he neared the strange city—still entirely alone and exhausted unto death.

" 'The traveller thought, "Perhaps my friend came to meet me by another route. There are probably several which lead from his city to mine! Since he did not come upon me, he will have turned around."

" 'When he saw the houses and gardens of the city before him in a shimmer of white and green, the heaviness vanished from his limbs, and he strode more quickly. He discovered without difficulty some one who knew the way to his friend's house; it was a magnificent dwelling in a well-to-do street. He entered and found the hall in which he walked filled with heavy and exceedingly valuable furniture but empty of men. "Strange," he thought, "that my friend also does not await me here. Could my letter have gotten lost or could the messenger have deceived me?" He sat down and waited.

" 'Meanwhile his friend sat above in the top floor of his great house surrounded by his books and his account tables.

" 'His head was buried in his hands. For days his soul had fought a difficult battle. When he had received the letter from the friend of his youth, that hour had come to his mind when the other had divided all his property with him for the love of their childhood days when they were as brothers. And he understood that now it was his turn to do the same. But now his nature, which had once sprung forth pure and kind from the hands of the Eternal, had become troubled in that period when from sudden poverty he had quickly returned to wealth. There was in him, at first, an anxiety about again becoming impoverished, later a love of possession which grew to a cold avarice. And now everything in him resisted the thought of separating himself from a part of what he owned.

" 'He decided finally to refuse to give him any gift. When he considered, however, that at the sight of his friend all his hardness might melt, he was overcome by anxiety. He commanded his servants to show the man out of the house.

[*168*]

" 'When now one of the company of servants entered, the waiting man gave him his name and asked for the master. Hearing the name, the servant did as he was ordered and turned him out. The poor man went from there to a place where he might be alone with his soul. There he cried his heart out to God. In that hour, in the midst of his bitter weeping, exhausted by the long journey without rest and refreshment, he expired.

" 'A few days later the rich man also passed away. They stood together before the Judge of the world. The poor man had won out of suffering and kindness an existence in great glory, but the rich man was condemned to sink to that place where ice burns like fire and the hard hearts have their dwelling.

" 'When his comrade learned of the judgement, he cried out amid tears, "Lord, the light itself that proceeds from Thee cannot illuminate the dark sorrow that I must feel through all eternity if this man must enter into the kingdom of torments."

" 'The voice from above said to him, "What do you request for the two of you?" "Grant, O Lord, that we may once again descend to the world," he answered. "Let him be born in wealth and me in poverty. I shall appear to him in the form of a beggar and will demand back what he owed me and refused me in that past life. But if his spirit is miserly, as it was then, I will pour glowing tears over his heart, and I will wrestle with his stubborn soul in order to attain that gift from him, be it farthing by farthing."

" 'Then the voice allotted the two of them a new return.

" 'The hard-hearted man lived a sumptuous life in an expensive house, the other grew up among needy people in a distant land.

" 'Now, O friend,' admonished the Baal-Shem, 'strain your soul and listen carefully to me!

" 'What had befallen both of them before this life neither of them knew. It happened that because of his need the poor man went travelling in order to beg, and thus came into the city where the other spent his days in worldly joy.

" 'The poor man wandered through the streets and came to the house of the rich man. Here he halted and raised his hand to the knocker to strike the door. At that moment a man came along the way, caught sight of a beggar at the gate and called to him, "Here you knock in vain; no one has ever gone from this house comforted." Then he knew that he would be refused aid and his hand fell down, but something in his heart said to him that he must reecive alms here and nowhere else. So he knocked, went before the master of the house and requested of him a small charity wherewith he might still his gnawing hunger. "If you do not give it to me, then I shall die," he said. "You hold my life in your hands."

" 'The rich man distorted his face to a laugh and jeered, "Save your energy and do not talk long! Every child on the street knows that I give no alms. I shall not break my custom for you."

" 'Then the poor man felt a rare strength arise in him; it seemed to him as if he were asking for more than his life. Strange, powerful words came forth out of his mouth, he employed forceful gestures and he beset the locked heart with all of his might.

[*170*]

" 'When the rich man felt so great a power storming down on him, he was seized by rage. He struck the beggar loose, and the poor man, who had concentrated his last strength in his asking, sank down dead under the blow.

" 'Now friend,' said the Baal-Shem, 'you have heard me to the end. Is there even now really nothing at all that you lack?'

"Then the Jew fell on his knees weeping before the master. 'Rabbi, I am that wicked man. You have torn off the veil of the ages, my eyes have gazed across the chain of happenings. What shall I do to purify the soul that I have corrupted?'

" 'Go and see in every poor man on the way a child of the beggar whom you have struck dead,' answered the Baal-Shem. 'Give as much as you can of your goods and of your help. Let your soul inundate the gift with love!' "

This is what Rabbi Shalom of Kaminka told the zaddikim who had gathered in Ropshitz for the anniversary.

From Strength to Strength

In the days of the Baal-Shem there lived two friends. They stood in that most beautiful time of youth when the last dawn still glows in heaven, enchanting and undefined: auroral dreams still hover near by, but soon the sun will draw near, the stern master, and his kingdom of forms will become visible.

Often the friends sat together, leaning against the bare wall of their little room, and talked of the meaning of life. To one of them the world was revealed through the word of the Baal-Shem. From each thing he received a message, and with every action he gave a response. He threw himself down on the green field, greeted the wind and the water and the beautiful animals that glided swiftly by, and his greeting was a prayer. Thus for him the meaning of life was founded in the Creator. His companion flew into a passion against him and declared that all this was a sin against the spirit of truth. For each thing has many surfaces and each creature many forms, but he who submits himself to a faith now sees of the multiple reality only one surface and one form; his way becomes at once secure and impoverished, and the search for truth, for the meaning of life, dies away in him. To this the other replied that in the world of enlightenment there are no surfaces and forms, rather each thing and creature stands there in its purity. Thus the friends often argued with each other.

Then it happened that a serious illness overtook that youth who was devoted to the Baal-Shem. In the pitiless intensity of the pain he recognized the message of a power which must bring his earthly life to its end. So he did not resist it, but rather yielded himself to the mighty element. Nonetheless, horror lay encamped on the road to that which would take place in the abyss of eternity. He let the Baal-Shem know that he was preparing himself for death, and when the master stood by his bed, he said, "Rabbi, how and by what means shall I proceed? A horror lies before me and disturbs my peace."

The Baal-Shem took the hand of the sick boy in his hands and said to him, "Child, recall: have you not always gone from strength to strength and from goal to goal? So you shall also move onward in the gardens of eternity." He touched the forehead of the sick boy and said to him, "Because the hour of the last dawn is still over you, and because you have lived in it genuinely and have not been afraid of its happiness, I shall write my sign on your forehead so that no one can terrify your way and hinder your path. So go hence, child, when death summons you." He bent over him, laid forehead on forehead, and blessed him.

When the master had gone, the other youth slipped into the room and knelt by the bed. He kissed the hand of the sick boy and said, "My beloved, they wish to take you away, and I know that you do not resist. Recall how we used to talk with each other among the birches of a summer evening, and finally you said only, 'Yes, it is,' and I said, 'No, it is not.' Now I am terribly frightened, for you are going away from me, are willingly going away with these, your eyes. My beloved, the birches are in your eyes, and also the summer evening. And everything says, 'Yes, it is.' I feel that it is, I myself say it, indeed, and know it too, for otherwise there were no meaning in everything, and yet you are going away from me. Whither are you going?" He sobbed over the hand of his friend and kissed it again and again.

The dying boy spoke, "Dear one, I go farther on the way. When I am on the way, I shall think of you and of our love. I will come to you to tell you of my path. Give me your hand."

Then the other cried out, "You shall not go, I shall keep you, you shall not go!"

But the dying boy spoke out of his peace, "Not so, you cannot strive against the Lord. You shall hold my hand until my pulse ceases to beat, and this is my promise to you that I shall return to behold the beautiful earth and you."

The gates of the firmament opened before the sign on his forehead as he ascended. He moved from goal to goal and from holiness to holiness and received the meaning of life. Time grew still and there was no space, only the way of becoming without place and lapse of time.

Suddenly his step was checked, time roared in his ears, and space struck him with cruel fists. Then he stood there in the midst of silent watchmen. He showed them the sign on his forehead. But they stared at him and shook their heads, and he knew that his forehead no longer bore a sign. Human despair threatened to overcome him, but he withstood it. Then he saw an old man before him who asked, "Why do you halt here?"

"I can go no farther," he answered. "This thing is not good," said the old man. "For if you tarry here, then the life of the spirit will abandon you and you will remain here as an unfeeling stone. For all the life of the world to come is this: to move from strength to strength unto the abyss of eternity."

"What can I do?" the youth asked him.

"I shall go into the sanctuary," replied the old man, "and find out why this has happened to you." He went, came back, and said, "You promised your friend that you would come to him and tell him of your way. You have forgotten to do this and have broken your promise. Therefore, the sign has been removed from your forehead and you have been prevented from entering the sanctuary of truth."

Then the youth beheld his friend on earth and grieved at having forgotten him. "What shall I do in order to free myself from my guilt?" he asked.

The old man answered, "Descend into the nightly dream of your friend and tell him what he desires to know."

The youth descended to earth and entered into the dream of his friend. He strokèd the forehead of the sleeping man and whispered in his ear, "Dear one, I have come to tell you of my way. But do not be angry at me for having delayed so long. For how can one think of a man, even though he be the most beloved, in the midst of the terror of God's vortex that overflows all limits?"

But the other rose up in his sleep, pressed his hand to his eyes and hissed forth the words of his chagrin from out of clenched teeth, "Depart from me, lying image, I will no longer let myself be made a fool of by you. I have waited and waited, and the promised one did not come. And now my spirit is rotted by waiting so that night after night your phantom visits me. But now I will no longer let myself be made a fool of. I command you, dissolve and appear to me no more!"

Then the youth threw himself trembling on his companion and clung to him. "Truly, I am no phantom, but your friend," he said, "and I have come to you out of the world of being. Think how we sat among the birches of a summer evening. Think how our right hands clasped each other in the hour of my death."

But the dreamer shouted, "You say the same night after night, and you catch me and I lift myself to you, then you vanish into the shadows. So let go of me now. See, I free myself from you!"

Once more the dead youth strove with his friend and cried, "Did not you say yourself, 'Yes, it is'?"

But the other only laughed in a hard voice, "Indeed I spoke thus, and I also waited. But the promised one did not come, and now I know that I was the plaything in the hand of a cruel hour. It was this hour that enslaved me and

shamed me and brought the yes of betrayal to my lips. But
I cry out against you, 'No, it is not!' "

Then the youth yielded and turned to disappear, but a
last hope came to him and out of the faint distance he called
to his comrade, "Then I will return in broad daylight and
bring you a sign."

In the upper world he hurried to the temple of truth,
sought out the old man and questioned him, "Help me and
say what sign I can bring my friend to show that it is
really I?"

"On this too I shall give thee counsel, my son," answered
the old man, "and God be with thee. At noon of every
Sabbath the Baal-Shem preaches on the mysteries of the
teaching in the house of study that stands in the heaven of
holy knowledge. And at the third Sabbath meal which unites
heaven and earth he preaches on these mysteries before the
ears of men, after his word has received the consecration
of the upper world. Therefore, go at noon of the Sabbath
and listen to the speech of your master in heaven; then
descend to your friend and report to him the speech. This
then will serve him as a sign; he will come to the holy meal
in the house of the Baal-Shem and receive the word out of
his mouth."

The youth did as he was advised, he absorbed the speech
of the master, descended, entered into the day-dream of his
friend and poured out the word over him like a balm. After
that he bent over him and kissed him, mouth on mouth, with
the kiss of heaven. Then he fled.

The other arose at once, and it seemed to him as if he
had experienced the unexperienceable. He went outside;

there stood the birches in the midday sun. He sat for a long time under the birches like one who knows.

When the sun began to sink, he went to the house of the Baal-Shem, not out of doubt but out of yearning. Now he stood in the door and heard the words out of the mouth of the Baal-Shem. He bowed himself at the feet of the speaker and said, "Rabbi, bless me for I want to die. For what is there left for me here?"

"Not so," replied the master. "Go outside to the birches that again stand in the summer evening and speak to them in your joy, 'Yes, it is.' And I do indeed bless you, but not for death, rather that now and here you may move from goal to goal, from strength to strength, and thus for ever and ever.

The Threefold Laugh

On a Friday evening, when the Baal-Shem sat with some
of his disciples at table and had just spoken the blessing
over the wine, it happened all at once that his face shone
with a joyful light as from within, and he began to laugh
and laughed much and in a hearty manner. The disciples
glanced at one another and looked around the room, but
there was nothing there that could have been the cause of
his laughter. After a short while the Baal-Shem laughed a
second time in the same manner, with the unexpected gaiety
and brightness of a child. Then a short while elapsed, and
his laugh rang out for a third time.

The disciples sat silent around the table. In their eyes this
occurrence was a rare and incomprehensible thing. For they
knew the master well and knew that he did not lightly sur-
render himself to such an impulse. So they suspected a significant ground for this joyousness and would gladly have

known it, yet none found the courage to approach the Baal-Shem about it. Therefore, they turned their eyes to Rabbi Wolf who sat in their midst, that he should inquire of the master the cause of his laughter. For it was the custom that at the end of the Sabbath Rabbi Wolf should go to the Baal-Shem when he rested in his room in order to learn from him what might have taken place in the course of the Sabbath.

Thus it happened this time too, and this disciple questioned him about the meaning of his laughter of the day before.

"Well now," said the Baal-Shem, "you would like to know from whence joy flowed into me. Come with me and you shall hear." Then he bid the servant harness the horses in order to take a drive in the open country, as was the custom after the expiration of the Sabbath. He climbed into the coach with his disciples, and they did not return home after a few hours as usual, but rather drove silently through the darkness the whole night. In the morning they reached a village. The Baal-Shem had the carriage stop at the house of the leader of the community. Soon his arrival was known to all the Jews. Everyone came and surrounded the house in order to do him honour. But he commanded the leader to send for Shabti, the bookbinder.

The leader replied, a little dissatisfied, "Master, what do you want with this man, who lives in our community without being especially noticed by anyone? He is an honest Jew, but never have I heard him praised for the sake of even the slightest learning. What good can he be to you?"

"Nevertheless," said the master, "it is my wish that you call him for me." He was sent for, and he came—a modest, grey-haired old man. The Baal-Shem regarded him and said, "Your wife too should come," and she also was soon present.

"Now," said the Baal-Shem, "you shall tell me what you did on the night of the last Sabbath. But say the simple truth, have no shame and hide nothing from us."

"Sir," Shabti answered, "I shall conceal nothing from you, and if I have sinned, then you behold me ready to accept penance at your hands as if it came from God Himself.

"All the days that heaven has given me, I have been able to live by my work; indeed, in good seasons I was able to lay aside a little savings for myself. But from the beginning it was my custom that my wife should go out at noon of the fifth day of the week to buy with great care all the necessities for the Sabbath—our wants in flour, meat, fish, and candles. After the tenth hour of the day before the Sabbath, I left my work and went to the prayer house to remain there until after the evening prayer. I have done this since my youth.

"But now, since I am beginning to age, my wheel of fortune has turned; my possessions have flown out of my hands, and my strength for work has been lamed. Now I live a life of care, and often I do not succeed in providing for all the needs of the Sabbath by the fifth day. My consolation is that whatever else may come, one thing I do not need to give up: ending my week's work on the tenth hour of the day before the Sabbath, entering the prayer house, and remaining there until evening speaking the holy psalms and the festive songs.

"On the tenth hour of the day before this Sabbath, I did not have a farthing in my hands to supply the wants of the holiday, and my poor wife did not have a pinch of flour in the bin. Yet I have never in all the days of my life required assistance of other men, and I wanted to get through this day too without alms. So I decided to fast during this Sabbath. But I feared that seeing no light burning on the table would weigh on my wife's heart all too heavily and that she might accept a candle and some Sabbath bread or a little fish if a well-meaning neighbour offered it to her. Therefore, I demanded of her that she not take help from any man, even though he pressed her to do so. For understand, Master, that the Jews among whom we live are of a kind disposition and would find it difficult to accept our Sabbath table's standing empty. My wife promised to do as I asked. Before I went to the prayer-house, I said to her, 'Today I shall tarry until the day declines. For if I should go home with the others from the prayer-house and they should see no light in my house, they would ask me the cause, and I would not know how to answer them. But when I come then, my wife, we shall receive with love what heaven will allot us.' Thus I spoke to my old spouse to comfort her.

"She, however, remained and cleaned the house in every nook and cranny. Since the hearth was cold and she had no food to prepare, she had a lot of time on her hands which she did not know how to spend otherwise, so she opened an old chest and took out the yellowed clothing of our youth in order to brush it and neatly put it in again. There she found, under all the old, worn-out clothes, a sleeve that we had missed once years ago and that since then had never been found. On the piece of garment there were some buttons in the form of little flowers, made out of gold and silver wire, a charming ornament such as one is likely to find on old clothes. These my wife cut off and took to the goldsmith and he gave her so much money that she was able to purchase the food that was needed for the Sabbath and also two good, strong candles and, in addition, even what we needed for the next day.

"In the evening when all the people had gone, I walked slowly through the streets to our house and saw already from a distance a light burning. The candlelight appeared festive and cozy. But I thought, 'My old wife has acted in the manner of women and could not refrain from accepting something.' I entered and found the table fully set and ready with Sabbath bread and fish, and I also found there wine over which to say the blessing. But I restrained myself from getting angry since I did not want to break the Sabbath. So I held myself back, spoke the blessing and ate of the fish. After that I said to my wife—but I spoke in a soft voice, for her poor, troubled soul moved me to pity—'It turned out then that your heart was not in a condition to accept hardship.' But she did not let me speak to the end, rather said in a bright voice, 'My husband, do you still remember the old material with the gold and silver buttons that we have been missing for years? When I cleaned out the great chest to-day, I found it. I gave the buttons to the goldsmith, and with the money I provided for the Sabbath.'

[*183*]

"Master, when I heard that my eyes filled with tears, so great was my joy. I threw myself down and thanked the Lord that he had remembered my Sabbath. I looked at my wife and saw her good face beam back my joy. Then I became warm, and I forgot the many wretched days. I seized hold of my wife and danced with her around the room. After that I ate the Sabbath supper, and my mood became ever lighter and more thankful; then I danced in joy and laughed a second time, and when I had consumed dessert, I did the same for the third time. You see, Master, so great was my happiness that this blessing had come to me from God alone and not from men. My joy was too great for me to be able to hide my feelings. It was in my mind to do reverence to God thereby, but if, Rabbi, it was an unworthy piece of foolishness that I danced thus with my wife, then give me a merciful penance, and I shall not fail to perform it."

Here Shabti the bookbinder ceased speaking. The Baal-Shem said to his disciples, "Know that all the hosts of heaven rejoiced with him and turned round with him in dance. And I, who saw all this, was moved to laughter the three times." Then he turned toward the two of them and said, "A child of your old age will be born to you who are childless. Call him Israel after my name."

Thus it happened. This boy became the Maggid of Kosnitz, the great man of prayer.

The Language of the Birds

Rabbi Arye, the preacher of Polnoy, nourished a burning desire for a wisdom that is so rare among mortals that in each age only one single individual is its heir and guardian. In the days when Rabbi Arye walked the earth and struggled for its possession, it was the Baal-Shem who was the master of it.

The bearer of this wisdom could understand the language of all creatures. He perceived what the animals on the earth and in the air confided to one another about the secrets of their existence; indeed, even what the trees and plants spoke to one another was known to him. If he laid his ear to the black earth or to the bare rock, the whispering of the creatures who shun the light and dwell in crevices and caves reached him.

Now Rabbi Arye was well aware of what presumption concealed itself in his wish. Still he imagined that he might for all that cherish it, for the sake of the noble striving out of which it was born to him. Already able, as an orator, to ravish men through his words, he believed that if the language of the creatures became a part of his own, he would preach out of the spirit of earth and of heaven and lead all souls to the Lord of creation. So he decided to journey to the Baal-Shem of whose friendly reception he could be sure and ask him to initiate him into the wonderful art. He believed that because of his high goal, the master would not deny him his request.

Wish and hope gave wings to his feet. So he went his way enveloped in his dream without noticing men or things. And thus he entered the room of the master. The chamber was full of men who listened attentively to the words of the Baal-Shem. Rabbi Arye closed the door behind him and silently bowed. When he lifted his head, his glance, harshly glittering from his restless desire, sank into the mildly shining eyes of the master. The Baal-Shem stood opposite him, leaning against the wall and speaking. The rabbi knew from his look that he had undoubtedly seen him, although the holy man did not show it by word or sign. So he remained standing at the door. He perceived that the master spoke in parable, but he was in no condition to follow the talk, for it cut him to the quick that the Baal-Shem did not even nod a passing greeting to him. Yet he bridled his impatient thoughts and made up his mind to wait composedly until the master should have finished, for he would certainly then bid him welcome.

But the Baal-Shem had spoken, and now let one person and another from the circle of hearers give utterance to his

thoughts; for while talking he had read from their counte-
nances what each one among them felt, whether disagree-
ment, question, or assent. While statement and counter-
statement were being heard, neither the host nor his guests
paid any attention to the new arrival, and thus he still stood
at the door, sorrowful unto death. The shame at seeing himself so disregarded nearly took his breath away. He felt as
if he must quietly slip away in order to cry his heart out
somewhere. But when his hand was already placed on the
latch in order to press it down noiselessly, he thought of the
longing that had brought him there, his constant wish
flamed up and mastered him, and he decided that no disgrace could be so bad that he would not suffer it for the
sake of his goal.

Meanwhile, many of the guests turned to leave. The host
conducted them to the door, bestowing on them the greeting of peace. Then, as his cloak grazed the rabbi, he turned
his head toward him almost imperceptibly and greeted him
over his shoulder as it were, in a level voice without joy or
warmth. The preacher's spirits had by now sunk quite low.
He felt as if he had been deprived of the ground on which
he stood. Yet his longing awoke once again and enlivened
him anew, he pulled all of his strength and patience together
and thus armed himself against the wrong that this day had
brought. He said to himself, "Whether it is a cruel accident
that has shamed me so or a trial that the master has devised
as suitable for my purification, I shall remain and wait the
gracious hour." So until late afternoon he spent the day in
the house of the Baal-Shem among the friends and disciples.

Toward evening the master had carriage and horses made ready for a drive, for he proposed to set out on a journey still that same day. Despair had already overtaken Rabbi Arye at the master's shunning him so, when the latter with a friendly movement of his hand called him over and invited him to join several other men who were accompanying him on this journey. Then the preacher's face trembled with joy, for he knew that the holy man chose with care companions for his trips to whom he planned to communicate his will or his knowledge. He was convinced that the master intended to grant him his desire on the way.

Silently the companions drove forth in the already darkening country-side. When now after sunset all the odours of the plants and the vapour of the earth more sharply and pungently scented the air, expectation mounted in the souls of all; for on this journey which the master undertook with his disciples, significant things usually happened. White mists in strange shapes arose out of the fields along the way and threw themselves against the carriage, increasing the shudder of presentiment of those who sat within. It grew dark, the horses galloped faster, everything swam together before them.

After the first enchantment, Rabbi Arye had fallen into a torpor. He forced his eyes to remain open, for he believed that the master might at any moment call his name in order to talk with him about that for which he yearned. Yet the Baal-Shem remained in wordless absorption. About midnight he bid the carriage halt before an inn in a small town on the way. The master immediately mounted the stairs to the upper chamber where the innkeeper had prepared for him a resting-place. The followers remained in a body in the large hall on the ground-floor. A servant girl hurriedly got ready the necessary beds by laying some cushions and covers on the benches against the wall. Everyone threw himself down exhausted and went to sleep.

Rabbi Arye lay down with the others, but as soon as his body touched the couch, the crippling lassitude which had tormented him on the trip was gone. His thoughts flew upward in a whirl, and his constant wish revolved in the centre of them. He strained himself to listen to every sound in the house. Now, while all slept, would the master call him to his chamber in the most mysterious hour of the night in order to bestow upon him the revelation? Thus he lay glowing with fever and awaited the morning.

While the shadows of night paled from a deep black into a fallow grey, he became aware of a stir on the floor above him and recognized the step of the master. Then a door was softly opened, and a stillness followed as before. The preacher lay awhile and listened; then impatience mastered him, he crept past the sleepers and hurried up the stairs since he was now certain that the Baal-Shem, who always renewed the springs of his life through a short sleep, had forsaken his bed. And Rabbi Arye imagined that this night-born hour of the oncoming day would be favourable to his request.

On the last step of the stairs he was met by so strong a light that he reeled backward and clung to the railing with his eyes closed. When he was in a condition to keep his eyes painfully open, he perceived the holy man in the opening of his chamber door, and the countenance of the Baal-Shem was the core of that fiery brilliance which had thrown him back a moment earlier. Blue silvery streams seemed to break forth from his eyes. The sight was of such a nature that a trembling weakness beset the preacher in all his limbs. He threw himself down on the last step. When he again dared to look, the face of the master resembled a paling star which yields before the light of day. After a while the Baal-Shem called him by name. He raised himself from his knees and hurried to the master with face cast down, there threw himself to the floor again and burst into tears. "Friend, what do you desire of me at this hour?" asked the holy man. The preacher could find no word in reply. "Do not be afraid, get up!" the master encouraged him, yet when the rabbi tried to speak, only a fresh stammering broke forth from his lips. Then he arose, distressed and ashamed, and left the master. He went softly to his companions below, who were still too imprisoned in morning sleep to hear his coming, and again sought out his bed. He had breakfast with them, sat uncommunicative in the midst of their conversation, and did not betray by any syllable the event of the night. But the Baal-Shem was as tranquil and in the centre of life as ever.

When they departed, the Baal-Shem called the preacher over and said to him, "Friend you shall take the place at my side."

So they drove into the noisy, busy day. When the small town lay behind them and the fields of the country stretched out to where a distant wood grew dark before the blue of heaven, the Baal-Shem bent forward and looked into his neighbour's eyes with a smile. "The reason for your arrival and for your stay in my house is known to me," he said. "You hoped that I would initiate you into my knowledge so that your ear, like mine, would be open to the language of all creatures. It is this, I know, that has led you to me." Rabbi Arye seized the hand of the master and laid his glowing face on it, but no answering sound came from his lips. But the Baal-Shem gazed out at the tender green fields of corn, and the smile remained on his countenance. After a time he spoke again, "Sit nearer to me and bend your ear to my mouth: I shall now, indeed, teach you my wisdom. But before I initiate you into the primal ground of the mystery, it is necessary that I bring to your attention a matter of which you know. Bear in mind, however, that what I shall now say to you is only the preparation for the final revelation.

"You know of the eternal carriage that stands in the highest sphere of the upper world. On each of its four corners there is the head of a creature—a man, a bull, a lion, and an eagle. These four creatures conceal in themselves the root and origin of all that which takes place, wins breath, and is born as word in the living being of our world. From the human countenance comes to us the spirit of speech which we exchange here below into a product of man. Out of the head of the bull comes the meaning of the sounds of those animals that are subject and helpful to us; out of that of the lion the significance of the cries that the wild and unrestrained animals in the forests and deserts send forth to call and lure one another; but the head of the eagle engenders the sounds of the feathered folk with which the air under heaven is filled.

"And know this, friend: he who is able to extend his soul so high that it penetrates into that sphere of the upper world in which the carriage stands and who then sees with such clarity and depth that he apprehends the mystery of the four creatures of the carriage, to him the meaning of all the sounds on the earth is revealed. He distinguishes the false word from the true and the deceitful tone from the heartfelt. He hears the voices under the earth conversing in the nights when to the human race the silence seems complete and every sound appears to have died away. The voices of the animals on the earth and the birds in the air convey to him those secrets which the senses of man ordinarily cannot perceive. Thus for him the world is never silent. It presses forward to him with every wonder; nothing is unyielding and nothing denies itself to him, for he has beheld the origin in the carriage above. But pay close attention, for what I shall now say to you is the heart of the revelation itself. Therefore, bend your ear close to my mouth and listen to me with your whole soul. Shut yourself off in this moment from all that exists, outside of you and my words!" And now he whispered to Rabbi Arye exalted and unheard-of things that the mysteries of the carriage and its figures would disclose to him. It seemed to him as if gate after gate sprang open before him, all shadows retreated, all that was murky became clear.

As he sat thus, pressed close to the master with one ear near his mouth, immersed in listening, the carriage entered a forest. The path was barely broad enough for the stately vehicle and the pine needles of the trees grazed one of his ears. Thus he became a little aware of the place and noticed that all kinds of birds were performing their morning song in a most charming manner. Wonderfully enough, he soon distinguished individual words and sentences. The whole was a great conversation, and everything had a gay, lovely meaning. Then the preacher was joyous and proud of heart, he eagerly listened further and presently also distinguished the voices of other animals and the content of their talk, and he was immensely gratified by his wonderful new faculty. But he by no means relinquished the one for the other; rather with his other ear he hearkened no less eagerly to the word of the master, and thus took in both with divided mind.

The forest cleared, and already they could see before them the city which was the goal of their journey. The Baal-Shem had now finished his instruction and glanced inquiringly at the preacher. "Have you mastered well what you have learned from me?" he asked after awhile.

Rabbi Arye looked at him radiantly with self-assured eyes. "Yes, Master," he replied. "I have understood everything well!"

Then the Baal-Shem passed the palm of his hand lightly over his forehead.

Now the rabbi forgot all, all that the Baal-Shem had revealed to his spirit. He sat there, inconsolably empty and as if burnt out, listened to the birds chirping in the furrows and understood of it as little as he ever had before this day—it was nothing but an animal's simple, senseless sound!

But the Baal-Shem smiled and said, "Alas for you, Rabbi Arye, you have a greedy soul! Could you not devote your soul to me entirely in the moment when I wished to instil the knowledge into it? Alas for you, friend, you wanted to enrich yourself immoderately and in haste! God's wonders are for those who can collect themselves in one thing and be satisfied in it."

Sobbing, the preacher hid his face in his hands.

The Call

Rabbi David Firkes the silent, the disciple of the Baal-Shem, wanted to call down the Messiah. He wished to make a storm-wind out of his will which would attack the upper gates, would rush and call and seize and draw to earth. He freed his life from all beings and powers, mortified himself and lived in detachment many days and nights. But soon he became aware that he was alone. He ought to speak for the age, but he was not able to. He should announce its ripeness, but he did not perceive it. The camp of men spread itself out far from him.

Then Rabbi David discovered what he must do. Each year on the Day of Atonement he was summoned to speak the great prayer before the community. Now for the first time he understood its meaning. He knew that he would bear on the wings of his words the prayers of all, the prayer of the community and the prayer of all Israel—for is not the

prayer house of the Baal-Shem the centre of the spiritual
earth? And he determined to fling his word over the people
like a powerful net so that all fervour should be carried
away from its narrow individual aim and conducted to the
Messiah. He wanted to bind up the souls of Israel into a
striving band. Yes, he wanted to speak for the age. All
words should flow into his word and in it stream upward.
Yes, he wanted to announce the ripeness of the age. The
manifold should coalesce into a unity that knows no imper-
fection.

The Day of Atonement arrived and the community
gathered for the morning prayer. They stood like dead men
in the clothes of the dead and prepared themselves to look
into the eye of eternity. Only the master was missing. The
Baal-Shem was usually the first in the prayer house, like a
gate-keeper of God. Today he was late, and the company of
his followers awaited him full of anxiety, for they knew that
everything that he did took its meaning from the secret
happenings of the world. When the morning was already
brightening to day, the Baal-Shem entered softly and almost
hesitantly. He went past the congregation and looked at no
one, walked to his place, sat down and laid his head on the
prayer-desk. The people stood, looked at him, and did not
dare to commence the prayer. But he raised his head after
awhile, and his eyes blinked like one who tries to look into
the sun; then he lowered it and raised it again, and this continued for a time. After that he stretched himself like one
awakening who wishes to shake off from his limbs a dream
that has enveloped him, and he motioned that they should
begin the morning prayer.

When this had been spoken, however, and the community prepared itself with consecrated hearts for the great prayer that is called the *mussaf*, the master looked around him in a circle and saw them standing—a great company, dumb, in the clothes of the dead, ready for death as for life. And softly, word drawn forth after word, as out of the depths of death, he spoke to those who stood around him, "Who will lead the *mussaf* prayer?" And despite the fact that his words were almost inaudible, at that same instant an astonishment was enkindled in the community which noiselessly spread throughout the silent room. For all knew that this was the office of Rabbi David; he had been appointed by the master many years ago as God's servant in speaking aloud the high *mussaf* on the Day of Atonement and bearing the prayers which the community spoke along with him. Out of all the trembling hearts and from all the whispering lips he should bear upward the wishes and the entreaties freed from the shyness of the hearts and the lips. Nonetheless, none dared answer the holy man.

He asked again and again until one person said softly and hesitantly, "Rabbi David is still the one who prays!"

Then the Baal-Shem straightened himself up and turned toward the ark, before which Rabbi David stood unearthly pale and as if dead, and spoke to him with powerful scorn, "You, David, do you want to lead the *mussaf* prayer? You know nothing and you want to lead the *mussaf* prayer on Yom Kippur?"

Then they all stood dismayed, for they did not understand what was taking place, and each asked himself how it was possible that the master could abuse a man in such a manner, and particularly a zaddik and particularly on the Day of Atonement. But the terror was great, and no one said a word. Rabbi David, however, still stood rigid and erect before the ark, and he felt as if a cyclone bore him through the night; fists rose out of the whirlwind and struck him, and icy talons tore forth his soul and hurled it into the night. Thus he stood lost in empty space and was not aware of any time.

But suddenly the vortex retreated, he found himself standing before the ark, and heard a word of the Baal-Shem sounding across to him. The Baal-Shem spoke in a light voice, "Is there no one to lead the prayer? Well then, you lead it after all, Rabbi David!"

Then the tears rushed forth from Rabbi David, he wept and wept, and out of his weeping began to pray and prayed in great weeping, and his broken heart sent him tears and ever new tears. And the tears carried away with them in their stream his readiness and his great will and thereby took with them the kavana of his spirit, the fruit of days and nights, the tension of the infinite. He no longer felt and knew anything other than the suffering of his heart, and out of his heart's suffering he spoke to God and prayed and wept. And from his suffering the suffering of the community took fire and flamed upward. He who had spread a covering over the blemishes of his soul now drew it aside and showed God his wounds as to a doctor. He who had erected a wall between himself and men tore it down and suffered the pain of others in his own pain. And he whose breast was heavy because he could not find the word in it that would press forward to the heart of destiny now found it and breathed in freedom.

When the holy day was almost over and the last solemn tones of the *neïla* had subsided into the evening, Rabbi David stepped up to the Baal-Shem. He stood before him without being able to look at him and did not see the kindly face near his own. He only felt that he could no longer hold himself up, rather sank down before him and lay there a while silent and struggling. Finally he raised his eyes and spoke painfully, "Rabbi, what fault have you beheld in me?"

Behind him the community had assembled, and all awaited the word of the master; with eyes that prayer had calmed and purified they watched his mouth. "I find no fault in you, Rabbi," spoke the Baal-Shem. He laid his hands on his shoulders, bent over him like a father who blesses his son, and said a second time, "I find no fault in you." And as the other's sorrowfully waiting glance lifted itself to him, he spoke further, "O Rabbi David, you prepared and sanctified yourself and bathed your body in the fire of mortification and stretched your soul like a bow-string of kavana in order to call the Messiah." He paused, the other bowed his forehead, and the Baal-Shem spoke further, "O Rabbi David, you wanted to fling your word over the people of Israel like a net and make all wills subject to you in order to call the Messiah."

The forehead bowed lower. "O Rabbi David," spoke the Baal-Shem further, "do you imagine that your power can grasp the ungraspable? And even were it to press forward to the innermost heaven and clasp the throne of the Messiah, do you imagine that you could hold him as my hand grips your shoulder? Above the suns, above the earths Messiah changes into a thousand and a thousand forms, and the suns and earths ripen in face of him. Concentrated in his higher form, scattered in unspeakable distances, he everywhere guards the growth of the souls, from out of all depths he lifts up the fallen sparks. Daily he dies silent deaths, daily he springs up in silent births, daily he ascends and descends. When once the soul, slender and perfected, treads pure ground with pure feet, then his hour will throb in his heart, then he will divest himself of all manifestations and will sit on the throne, lord of the flames of heaven that have blazed up from the redeemed sparks, and he will descend and come and live and will bestow on the souls their kingdom."

And the Baal-Shem spoke further, "But you, Rabbi David, what have you done! You wanted to hurl both yourself and the community of Israel into the night for the sake of the morning. But do you know the lord of the night? Know that there is always one who questions the age and one who answers out of the age. One who wants to give and one who refuses to accept. This is the lord of the night, appointed for the purpose of announcing the need of the age. When he saw that you prepared and sanctified yourself, a great joy sprang up in him, and he planned to catch the prayer of Israel in your prayer and to make out of it a plaything for himself. He lay in wait for your prayer along the way in order to catch it. This morning I strove with him in order to drive him away, but I could not overpower him. Then I smote your soul with shame so that you gave up your will and burst forth in tears. Your prayer ascended

in the midst of the prayers of Israel, freely upward to God."
Then the forehead of Rabbi David bowed all the way to the
ground. But the Baal-Shem raised him up, drew him to himself and said, "When your weeping overcame you, the
suffering of Israel took fire from your suffering. Each stood
before God in the refining fire of his heart's suffering, each
became pure in the stream of his tears. How many fallen
sparks you have thereby elevated!"

The Shepherd

Always when the light sends forth its messenger, the night sends forth its messenger too. The light has only its glance, but the night has a thousand arms. The messenger of the light has only his deed, but the messenger of the night has a thousand gestures.

In those days it was called Jacob Frank. Well-versed in all of the arts of deception, he falsified the most holy, marched through the cities of Poland with twelve chosen ones and allowed himself to be venerated as the Messiah. A vari-coloured path of lies went out from him, his soft, glittering eyes intoxicated the land, and every wavering heart fell to him.

One morning the Baal-Shem felt a hand on his shoulder, and when he turned he saw the angel of battle with pale forehead and wrathful brows. "What do you want, Master?" he asked with uncertain voice.

But the other said, "You know what," and went. His hand had left the shoulder of the Baal-Shem, but a burden had remained and would not leave.

So the Baal-Shem prepared himself for battle. And since he saw that the strength that resided in him was not sufficient for this work, he decided to call home all the rays that he had ever bestowed on earthly beings. He summoned the rays from afar, threw a call over the earth, and said, "Come home, my children, for I need you for battle." Soon the ray-children had flown thither and surrounded him in a wide circle. Israel, the son of Eliezer, the Baal-Shem, gazed far out to where one self-illuminating sphere of his children enclosed another, as the setting sun contemplates its image on the rim of day, diffused to all distances in sunset glow. Then he spoke softly and slowly, "Once I sent you forth and bestowed you to bring comfort or joy or deliverance. But now I call you home that you may again be mine and help me in the great conflict with the messenger of the night. I would not have drawn you from the places of the world wherein you grow and awaken life if it were not a question of redemption and of the birth of the future. But now I summon you."

Then there was silence again over the land. Finally, a little spark said, "Forgive me, Master, and all of you forgive me for speaking to you of an unimportant matter. But it is this that I would ask you, dear Master, that you might allow me to return to my place. For when you sent me forth from out of yourself, you sunk me into the heart of a young man who gazed despondently from his window into a world that closed itself off from him. But since I have entered him, it has opened itself to him and become alive for him, and the hill before his window appears to him green and yellow and red and white, according to the play of the seasons. Would you deprive him of it?"

The Baal-Shem silently nodded permission to the spark. But immediately other voices were raised which told of the men whom they had freed from doubt and emptiness, from frenzy and bitterness, from blindness and need, and who, if they left them, must again sink down into the darkness. And soon there resounded through the air from a thousand mouths, "Would you spoil all that you have redeemed?"

"Well then, my children," he said smiling, "I bless you for a second time. Return home!" He arose and extended his hands over the luminous company.

When he was alone then and as far as the rim of heaven saw the last ray of gold flow back into the world, he addressed his soul, "Now seek for yourself companions, dear soul, who are enveloped and enclosed in their work as the resting bird in its soaring. Lay the command on their shoulders and guide them against the man of the thousand gestures that they may conquer him!" The Baal-Shem ascended into the upper world and entered the heaven of the prophets. There he found Ahia of Shilo, the ancient, once the envoy of divine wrath against the kings of Judah.

Ahia greeted him, "Blessed be he who comes, Israel my son. Thy wish flames up to me as brightly now as at the time when you were a boy and I descended to you in the nights to teach you the mystery of fervour."

"Much of the fervour from my heart's core has been sacrificed," replied the Baal-Shem, "and I no longer have enough for the deed. My wish, which you have perceived from my step, is to find those souls who breathe in their fire like a seraph. Their ardour shall consume the messenger of the night."

"He whom you seek is not among the souls in my realm," said Ahia. "Let us ask Elijah. He may well have beheld such a one on his travels over the earth."

They went to Elijah, who was just then passing with fleeting feet through the hall of the heaven of the prophets, his limbs still tense from flight yet already awaiting a new destination in his heart. As they approached him, he turned toward them. Before the question had yet left their lips, he said to the Baal-Shem, "He whom you seek is Moshe the shepherd. He pastures sheep in the mountains that are called the Polonian." And already Elijah inclined again toward his earth and prepared himself for a new trip.

The meadows undulated beneath the breath of summer. The Baal-Shem strode there, silently shut in himself. He did not heed the animals that came out of the wood with trusting eyes when they perceived his step and did not heed the twigs that caressed his arm. His feet did not feel the path. Thus he came to the great mountain meadow which, beginning behind a broad ditch, stretched upward in steep ascent unto the summit of the mountain. On the broad plains were scattered Moshe's sheep like a people of light, fleecy clouds. When the Baal-Shem beheld the meadow, he stepped behind a bush in order to look at the shepherd unobserved.

He saw a youth standing on the edge of the ditch; fair hair covered his shoulders, his eyes were wide open like a child's. A coarse garment covered his strong limbs. The youth opened his mouth and spoke. Although no one was before him and no one was in sight far and near, he carried on a dialogue with some one. "Dear Lord," he spoke, "teach me what I can do for you! If you had sheep that I could guard, I would attend them day and night without desiring wages. Show me what I shall do!" Then the moat came within his sight. Immediately he got up and with arms akimbo and feet close together began to leap over the ditch. The ditch was broad and full of slime and all kinds of crawling things, and the leaping cost the lad much sweat. Still he did not leave off and did not pause on one bank, rather leaped across and back and said in between, "For love of you, Lord, and to please you!" He only interrupted this action at times in order to look after the sheep which had in the meantime climbed all too high. He spoke affectionate words to the beasts and then he ran again to the ditch.

The Baal-Shem looked on this for a long time, and it seemed to him as if this service was greater than any that he had ever offered God out of a dedicated soul. Finally he came out of his hiding-place, went up to Moshe and said, "I have something to say to you."

"It is not permitted me," the shepherd answered, "for my day belongs to him who hired it."

"I just saw you leaping without thought of time," said the master.

"That I do for the sake of God," replied the shepherd, "and for Him I may lose awhile."

But the Baal-Shem laid a kindly hand on his arm, "Friend, I too have come to you for the sake of God."

Soon they sat side by side under a tree, and the holy man talked of his concern while next to him the shepherd listened with quivering soul.

The Baal-Shem spoke of the solitude of God and of God's presence that is exiled in the destiny of the imperfect world. He told how all creatures suffer in its separation and work toward its reunification. "It is," he said, "as if the mystery of eternity were already near and waiting to fulfil itself. But the demonic might that opposes the unification of heaven and earth has once again dispatched its messenger to hinder it. In luring darkness he moves through the world of men and seduces them through the false appearance of redemption."

When the Baal-Shem spoke of the messenger, the shepherd sprang to his feet and cried, "Master, where is this man of whom you speak? For it cannot be that he will survive the moment when I shall find him!" But the master bid him be silent and began to instruct him in battle.

The demon adversary, however, hovered invisibly in the air and became aware of the bond between the two. And since it was given him to see into the heart of events, he understood the meaning of the dialogue between the old man and the youth on this meadow at the edge of the forest. He extended himself over the world and with terrible power sucked himself fast to all the evil that thrived in that day. After that he fought his way into the upper realm and demanded in shrill words his right to the ages. Then there came out of the nameless centre of solitude a voice that was full and overfull with sadness. The demon fell back in terror. But the voice said, "The moment is yours and always only the moment until once knowledge conquers you and you plunge into my light because you can no longer bear to be the lord of the moment." The voice ceased speaking. But the demon shook off the fetters of knowledge, descended rapidly, seized the clouds and rolled them together with raging fists. He awakened the storm-wind, commanded the thunder to rumble and set free the lightning for its work. Fire fell in the city, and the bells groaned.

When Moshe the shepherd became aware of peal and din, he started up from the holy words and thought of his animals, which had been scattered unprotected over the mountain during the uproar of the heavens. He did not heed the holy man and his warning; instead he sprang up and with rapid strides hurried above to his sheep to lure back the stray ones with cajoling words.

Slowly, head and eyes bowed to the earth, the Baal-Shem descended. When he stood in the valley, he felt an arm around his neck. As he turned, he saw an angel with shining forehead who now also laid the other arm around his neck and kissed him. He recognized the prince of death and of rebirth.

GLOSSARY

GLOSSARY *

[Words followed by a dagger (†) are also explained in the Glossary.]

AFTERNOON PRAYER: *see* Minha.

AGGADA: Literally, "report," "information." A generic term for the narrative, interpretative, and instructive portions of the Talmud†. But it is also used for each individual portion of this type. Similarly the non-Aggadic portions of the Talmud are called Halaka, from Heb. "to walk"; "the way"; then, "law," religious practice.

AHIYA OF SHILO: According to legend, this prophet, who lived at the time of Solomon and Jeroboam, was the teacher of the Baal-Shem. While the latter was still a youth, Ahiya is said to have come down to him from heaven to instruct him in the mysteries.

BILBUL: Confusion, thus, false accusation, specifically, accusation of ritual murder.

BLESSING (Heb. Beraka): For many occasions and everyday activities, especially before the taking of food or drink, blessings are

* I wish to acknowledge my indebtedness to Dr. Leonie Sachs, who did the ground-work for the translation of this glossary.—Tr.

prescribed, the opening part of which is constant: "Blessed art thou, O Lord (our God, King of the Universe)," whereas the second part is adapted to the occasion. A blessing spoken outside of its prescribed occasion or without being followed by the activity for which it is intended, is a "vain blessing" (Heb. Beraka levatala) and is considered a violation of the Third Commandment (Exod. 20:7). *See also* Eighteen Benedictions.

BRIDAL CANOPY (Huppa): The wedding ceremony is performed in the open air under a canopy spread over four posters. Colloquially the word "Huppa" has become synonymous with "wedding."

CARRIAGE (Merkaba): Following the vision of God in Ezekiel, chapter 1, the mystery of God's Throne World has been symbolized, ever since Talmudic times, in the mystical image of the Carriage. (In the Talmud the esoteric teaching of the Throne of God is called *Maasse Merkaba*.)

CLOTHES OF THE DEAD: The death garments, a plain white linen gown, called "kittel," and a white cap, are made for the young Jewish man at the time of his wedding. In many regions it is customary for him to put them on for the first time at the marriage ceremony. The married man wears them on certain occasions, especially during the synagogue services on the Day of the New Year and the Day of Atonement†. The dead person is clothed in these garments and, wrapped in his prayer shawl, he is laid in his grave.

DAY OF ATONEMENT (Heb. Yom Kippur or Yom ha-Kippurim): At one time, the day on which the scapegoat was sent into the wilderness (Lev. 16) and the sacrificial ritual by the High Priest was performed. In Talmudic writings, Yom Kippur is often simply called "The Day," because on this day the process of the turning and regeneration of the soul, which began on Rosh ha-Shanah, the Holiday of the New Year†, reaches its height and completion. It is the day of the confession of sins and of purification, the day of strict fasting from one evening to the next. The synagogue service lasts from morning till night. The worshippers stand without shoes, dressed in white gowns resembling the shrouds of the dead. Before the Holy Day all men must forgive each other, because on this day only man's sins against God are atoned for, and not those against his fellow-men.

DAYS OF AWE (Yamim Noraim): also called Days of Judgment; *see* New Year, Holiday of.

DAYS OF JUDGMENT, DAYS OF MERCY: The "Days of Awe"; *see* New Year, Holiday of.

DAYS OF PENITENCE: *see* New Year, Holiday of.

EIGHTEEN BENEDICTIONS: called the Shemone Esre (i.e., Eighteen), also simply Tefilla (prayer), one of the oldest portions of the Prayer-Book. This prayer recurs in every service, morning, afternoon, and evening. It is spoken by each worshipper silently (because, according to the Zohar, it must be heard only by the angels in charge of receiving prayers—and who are therefore called "Ears"—whereas, if the prayer were caught by human ears, it would be prevented from rising), and it must not be interrupted by any profane word. Afterwards it is repeated by the precentor (for the benefit of those who are not familiar with this prayer).

ELOHIM: Biblical name for the One God. In its grammatical form, this word is the plural of a noun which, even in the singular, means "God." Despite its plural form, Elohim is usually treated grammatically as singular when it stands for the One God. This plural-singular designation, whose origin and importance for the history of religions have not yet been clarified, is experienced as a deeply significant mystery. God's "Names" are His manifestations, His "modes of action" (middot). Among these, the name Elohim denotes the "modes" of power and judgment, whereas the ineffable name, represented by the tetragrammaton YHVH, expressed the "mode" of mercy and compassion.

ETROG: "The fruit of goodly trees" (Lev. 23:40), the citron (often identified with "the golden apple"), over which a blessing† is said during the eight-day fall holiday of Succoth (Feast of Booths, or Tabernacles).

GEHENNA: Ge Hinnom, the "valley of Hinnom" near Jerusalem. According to II Kings 23:10, this was the valley where the (misnamed) cult of Moloch took place. Later this place name became the designation of "hell" (Greek Geenna).

GREAT CONFESSION: On the Day of Atonement, the "Eighteen Benedictions"† ("eighteen" here only in a symbolic sense) include the Great Confession of Sins. This is first spoken silently by the worshippers, but then, during the repetition aloud of the Prayer by the precentor, the Great Confession is solemnly spoken in unison by the precentor and the congregation.

HASID (plural: Hasidim): In the language of the Bible, *hesed* is God's loving-kindness toward His Creation, as well as man's devoted and open-hearted love toward God and his fellow-man (both belong together). Only in this all-inclusive sense can Hasid be understood to mean "pious." In post-Exilic Judaism, there sprang up, again and again, groups of people who called themselves Hasidim. They had in common the fact that they desired the realization of their piety, of their relation to the Divine, in this earthly life. This endeavor is especially manifest in the "Hasidic" movement founded by the Baal-Shem.

HOLY ARK (Aron ha-Kodesh): Curtained shrine, placed at the east wall of the prayer house and synagogue. In this shrine the Torah† scrolls are deposited from which the weekly portions are read. Symbolically the ark represents the Biblical "Ark of the Covenant," which constituted the central point of Holiness in the Sanctuary in Jerusalem, just as the prayers of the congregation represent the sacrificial service. The precentor (Heb. Shliah Tzibbur, literally, "emissary of the congregation") says the prayers standing at a pulpit placed in front of or next to the ark. Prayers of special sacredness are spoken before the opened ark.

IMMERSION BATH: *see* Ritual Bath.

ISAAC LURIA (Rabbi Yitzhak Ashkenazi, also called "Ari," i.e., lion, by reversing the initials of his title and name): Isaac Luria, around whom many legends have been woven, was the chief master of the later Kabbala†. He was born in Jerusalem in 1534 and died in Safed, where he had spent the last years of his life, in 1572. *See also* "Prayer-Book."

JACOB FRANK (1726–1791): Declared himself to be the Messiah and temporarily gained numerous followers, especially in Poland. After some vehement controversies with Judaism, Frank had himself baptized, as had many of his followers. Even after converting to Christianity, they continued as a sect, which, however, ceased to exist soon after Frank's death.

KABBALA: Literally, "what has been received through tradition"; more precisely, "knowledge to be transmitted only by word of mouth." It is the term used for the Jewish secret teachings, especially in their medieval forms. Proceeding from ancient mystical traditions, nourished out of gnostic sources, the Kabbala finally developed into the mystical theology of Judaism. It strove for the coherence of a system which interpreted this world from the perspective of the higher world. From the sixteenth to the eighteenth century, the Kabbala maintained its position as the dominant theology of Judaism, thereby providing to a large extent the theoretical foundation for Hasidism, especially the later, so-called Lurian version of the Kabbala, named after Rabbi Isaac Luria†.

KEDUSHA: Literally, "holiness"; then, "sanctification." Name given to the responsive prayer sung between the precentor and congregation, which is inserted in the service during the repetition of the Eighteen Benedictions† by the precentor, before the third Benediction. This prayer is based on the visions of heavenly beings by the Prophets Isaiah and Ezekiel ("We will sanctify thy name in the world even as they sanctify it in the highest heavens"). The main portions of the Kedusha are: Is. 6:3b (Trishagion) and Ez. 3:12b; in addition, verses taken from the Psalms and the Pentateuch. The Kedusha is never said by the individual worshippers, only by the congregation as a whole. It is an especially sacred portion of the synagogue service, sung in a loud voice, "with trembling and with fear."

KOL NIDRE: The opening words ("All vows") of the solemn formula of release from vows which have not been fulfilled and which cannot be fulfilled, spoken on the Eve of the Day of Atonement.

LETTERS OF THE ALPHABET AS ELEMENTS OF THE WORLD: The beginnings of this doctrine are already found in the Talmud ("Bezalel knew how to arrange the letters with which heaven and earth were created." Berakot 55). Later this doctrine was elaborated in the *Sefer Yetzira* (Book of Creation), the basic work of Jewish mysticism of numbers and letters, and from there taken over into the Kabbala†.

MAGGID: Preacher.

MAN OF THE LORD: Samuel; *see* I Sam. 9:6 ff.

MASTERS OF THE TALMUD: The Palestinian and Babylonian scholars who took part in the transmission and development of the teachings of the Talmud†, between the first and sixth centuries of the Common Era (called in Hebrew Rabbanan, "our masters," or just Hahamim, "sages").

MATZA: Unleavened bread eaten during the eight days of the spring feast of Pesach, commemorating the Exodus from Egypt; the Jewish feast of Passover. The preparation of the matzot is carried out with special consecration and care.

MEAL: "Holy Meal," "Third Meal," "Meal of Teaching." The third of the traditional meals eaten on the Sabbath†.

MESBITZ: Yiddish pronunciation of the town of Miedzyborz in Volhynia. Residence of the Baal-Shem after he had completed his wanderings.

MESSENGER OF THE CONVENANT: *see* Messenger of the Messiah.

MESSENGER OF THE MESSIAH, i.e., the Prophet Elijah: According to Jewish legendry, of which he has become the outstanding figure, the Prophet Elijah, who was carried up to heaven, has been God's constant messenger to mankind. He is present at every Jewish boy's entering into Israel's covenant with God. He is present also at every Seder table, in the evening of the Passover festival commemorating the great Act of the Covenant, the delivery from Egypt. At the Seder a special cup of wine is set aside for the Prophet. He gives help in need, guidance in uncertainty, and, as forerunner of the Messiah, as arouser and summoner, he is destined, in times to come, to prepare sluggish mankind for the coming of the Messiah. To partake of Elijah's visible appearance and of his message signifies the true initiation of a person into the mysteries of the Teaching.

MESSIAH (Greek form of the Hebrew word "Mashiah"): "The Anointed." The man anointed by God to be king of the world at the end of time. He will bring to an end the exile of Israel and administer the kingship of God, which will then be established over the entire world.

MINHA: Originally a special kind of offering (Lev. 2), later the afternoon prayer which took the place of the afternoon offering (Ezra 9:4).

MUSSAF: "Addition"; originally the special offering added on the Sabbath and on holidays; later the sequence of prayers taking the place of this offering and spoken on these days after the general Morning Prayer.

NEÏLA: "Closing"; the concluding prayers on the Day of Atonement, spoken "as the sun sets into the tree tops," "while the heavenly gate of Judgment and Mercy closes."

NEW YEAR, HOLIDAY OF (Heb. Rosh ha-Shanah; literally, "Head of the Year"): The two-day New Year Holiday, which occurs in the time between the first week of September and the first week of October, is the festival of the constant renewal by God of the world (created on this day) and of man's soul in a process of heart-searching and turning back to God, of judgment and mercy. This process begins on this day and ends ten days later (at the end of the "ten days of Penitence," or, "Days of Awe") on the Day of Atonement. In the school of The Great Maggid,* Rosh ha-Shanah was called the Head of the Year, because it was the moment of the conception of Creation. Yom Kippur was called the Heart of the Year, because it was the moment of elemental fulfillment. Before this Holiday period, every zealous Hasid used to travel to his Zaddik's town in order to be near him during the sublime hours.

NINTH OF AB: This day, occurring between the middle of July and the middle of August, commemorates the destruction of the first Temple by Nebuchadnezzar and of the second Temple by Titus. It is a day of mourning and fasting. In the synagogue services the Lamentations, ascribed to the Prophet Jeremiah, are recited. All lights are extinguished, except one for the precentor. The worshippers sit on the floor, their shoes

* Dov Baer of Mesritch, the chief disciple of the Baal-Shem.—Tr.

removed, like people in mourning. Likewise, the scanty last meal on the eve of the fast is taken while sitting on the floor, in silence.

PHYLACTERIES (Tefillin): Capsules containing four texts from the Torah written on parchment strips. As a symbol of the Covenant with God, these capsules are tied with straps around the left arm and onto the forehead on weekday mornings, as ordained in Deut. 11:18. On the Sabbath and on holidays such a testimony is not necessary.

PRAYER-BOOK (Heb. Seder ha-Tefillot, i.e., Order of Prayers; also called in short: Siddur, i.e., Order): Compilation of the daily prayers in their prescribed order. Although the various editions of the prayer-book show but slight deviations in the actual text of the prayers (those that do occur being due to differences in regional or congregational usage*), there arise considerable divergences because of the practice of accompanying the text with explanations and Kavanot, i.e., directions of religious intention. The Prayer-Book of Rabbi Isaac Luria† contains Kavanot of the Lurian imprint, which are held in the highest esteem by the Hasidim.

PRAYER SHAWL (Tallit): Rectangular prayer shawl or mantle resembling a toga (originally it was an Oriental outer garment), on whose four corners are attached the prescribed fringes (Tzitzit; Num. 15:37 ff.), and in which the men wrap themselves while praying.

RABBI: *see* Rabbanim.

RABBI AKIBA: One of the most influential and celebrated by legend among the early masters of the Talmud, the real founder of the Mishna. He helped Simon bar Kochba, the "Son of the Star," in his great revolt against the Roman emperor Hadrian (132–135 C.E.) and died a martyr.

RABBANIM: Plural of Rav (master), as well as of Rabbi (literally, "my master"). Both Rav and Rabbi are titles for religious teachers, Rav designating the religious judge and Rabbi the

---

* There are greater divergences between the prayer-books of the different branches of American Judaism.—Tr.

religious leader of the congregation, as indicated by the more personal form of address. However, the functions of the Rav and those of the Rabbi may at times be performed by the same person.

RETURN OF THE SOULS (Gilgul, i.e., cycle): Doctrine of the transmigration of souls, developed in the Kabbala† under Oriental influences, systematized chiefly by Isaac Luria† and from this source taken over by Hasidism. According to this doctrine, the souls, separated from their bodies by death, enter new bodies, not only human ones, but also animal, vegetable, or mineral ones. The soul may also enter a body which already has a soul (Ibbur, literally, "impregnation," "superimposition of souls"), sometimes in a beneficial fashion, only in order to perform a particular action, but frequently in a demonic manner, as Dibbuk ("clinging"), thus producing "possession."

RITUAL BATH: In order to regain "cleanness," immersion in flowing water is prescribed in many instances (Lev. 15:5 f.; Num-19:19; Deut. 23:12). The High Priest was enjoined to precede his ministrations on the Day of Atonement† with a ritual bath. The Hasidim re-instituted this immersion as a primeval symbol of re-birth. Ritual immersion in this interpretation was taken over into Kabbalistic practice from ancient traditions, especially those of the Essenes and the Hemerobaptists. The Zaddikim (see Zaddik) practiced immersion with a lofty and joyous passion, which was not of an ascetic nature. The meaning of this fervor is manifest in the words of one Hasid who said that "ritual immersion could be replaced with a spiritual act, that of casting off corporality."

SABBATH: The Sabbath is observed from sundown on Friday till sundown on Saturday. Hours before the beginning of the Sabbath, many pious Jews cease their work and, after taking the ritual bath† and donning a festive garment, prepare themselves in quiet meditation to receive the Sabbath "bride" or "queen." At nightfall the congregation gathers together for evening prayer, "to welcome the Sabbath" (Kabbalat Shabbat). The bridal symbolism appears in the song whose chorus reads, "Come, my friend, to meet the bride; let us welcome the countenance of the Sabbath." The evening service is followed by the first of the three traditional Sabbath meals. It begins with the blessings over the wine, the bread, and the Sabbath (Kiddush; actually, sanctification). The second meal follows the morning service, which includes the reading of the weekly portion from the Torah† and the Prophets and is extended by the Mussaf prayer†. The "Third Meal," following the afternoon service (*see* Minha), has been developed by the Hasidim in a special fashion. It is a communal meal taken at the Zaddik's† table. Thus it becomes the crystallizing center of Hasidic communal living, effecting renewal. The hight point of the "Third Meal" is the Zaddik's instruction in the Torah, rapturously received by his disciples. The ceremony of "separation" (Habdalah) concludes the Sabbath. In this ceremony—to test, as it were, distinction in one sense perception after another—first the blessing over the wine is said, then that over the spices, smelled at and passed around in the "Besomim box" (the spice receptacle); then, after having contemplated one's finger-nails at the light of the candle, one says the blessing over the flame. The ceremony is ended with the praise of God "who maketh a distinction between holy and profane." The Hasidim follow this with the "Farewell Meal for the Queen," which is accompanied with singing and dancing. On the Sabbath any kind of work is prohibited. But the concept of "work" is extended to include even activities which require no particular effort, such as the attending or use of fire, the use of any means of transportation, and even the walking beyond a certain distance from one's home (the Techum Shabbat, "Sabbath limit").

SANCTIFICATION OF THE NAME (Kiddush ha-Shem): This is the term designating every pious deed of man which helps to establish the kingdom of God on earth.

SHEKINA: "Indwelling," the "glory" of God, the Presence of God in the world. The Divine Being which does not dwell in the world but rests entirely in itself is called Elohut ("Divinity"), that is, the Divine side of God, in no way comprehensible by man. The Shekina, the Indwelling of God in the world, is also the suffering of God with the world. She follows her people into the dark realm of exile; along with Israel, the Shekina, too, undergoes exile. The man who within himself achieves unity between the sphere of thought and that of action works toward the unification between the realm of thought and the realm of action, that is, between God and His Creation, in which He allows His Shekina, His Glory, to dwell.

SHOFAR: Ram's horn which is blown in the synagogue, especially on Rosh ha-Shanah, in memory of the revelation on Mt. Sinai (Exod. 19:16), in anticipation of the Last Judgment (Zephaniah 1:16), for the awakening of the souls, and as a call to God. Likewise the awaiting of the Messiah is linked with the belief that at the time of his coming "The Great Shofar" will awaken and call together "the exiles from the four corners of the earth." This is why the ninth of the Eighteen Benedictions† spoken in the daily prayers reads as follows: "Sound the great horn for our freedom, lift up the ensign to gather our exiles, and gather us from the four corners of the earth. Blessed art thou, O Lord, who gatherest the banished ones of thy people Israel."

SIDE OF MERCY—SIDE OF JUDGMENT: *see* Elohim.

SIMEON BEN YOHAI: A master who lived in the second century of the Common Era and has been glorified by many legends. He was elevated by the Kabbalists to the stature of their central figure. To him was attributed the authorship of the chief Kabbalistic work, the Zohar. Sentenced to death by the Romans for his outspoken criticism, he lived hidden in a cave with his son for many years. Later he settled in the secluded town of Meron (near Safed), in the mountains of Galilee, where he taught and died. There his grave is still pointed out. Even today it is visited by pilgrims from all parts of the country on the anniversary of his death, which is commemorated with a hearty folk festival.

SPARKS (Nitzotzot): According to an ancient interpretation (*Bereshit Rabba* on Gen. 1:5 and 1:31), God created and rejected many worlds before creating ours. This was thought to be indicated in the verse, "And God saw everything that He had made, and, behold, it was very good." But only the Kabbala† gave to this pre-Creation a wider meaning than that of gradual perfecting. During "the breaking of the vessels," i.e., of the earlier chaotic worlds, which were incapable of holding Divine abundance, the Holy Sparks "fell into the shells," i.e., the dividing, hindering, demonic enclosures which alone are "evil." But they fell in order to be lifted up again: those worlds came into existence and ceased to exist in order that man might work toward Redemption.

TALMUD (Learning, Teaching): Canonical collection of the "oral teachings," which was compiled during the first centuries of the Common Era and has been handed down in two versions (see below). Judaism holds that, along with the "written Teaching" contained in the Bible, an "oral Teaching" had also been revealed, which, from Moses' time on, was transmitted by word of mouth from generation to generation. But each generation has to reacquire this oral tradition for itself by constantly checking it against the text of the "Scripture" (for whose interpretation in the tenor of the oral teachings special methods were developed). The first, earlier main part of the Talmud is the Mishna, literally "review," then "instruction" in general. It was compiled and edited between the last quarter of the first and the end of the second century of the Common Era, and is written in Hebrew. The second, far more extensive part of the Talmud is called Gemara (literally "completion," the finished study). The Gemara discusses and comments on the Mishna. Two versions of the Gemara have been handed down to us: that of the Jerusalem Talmud and that of the far more voluminous Babylonian Talmud. Both were compiled during the period up to the sixth century of the Common Era, the former written in Western Aramaic, the latter in Eastern Aramaic.

TORAH: "Instruction," Teaching, Law (that preserved "in writing" and that handed down "by word of mouth"). As a book, Torah means the Pentateuch. It is divided into weekly portions to be read before the congregation. Copies of the Pentateuch, written by hand on parchment, are kept in the "Holy Ark†." These scrolls consist of parchment strips, many yards long and attached with their narrow side to a pole around which the inscribed parchment is rolled.

WORLD TO COME (Heb. Olam Habba): The age inaugurated by the coming of the Messiah†.

ZADDIK (the proven one, the perfected one): In the Bible this word denotes the man perfected in righteousness. In the Kabbala, the Zaddik, in interpreting Prov. 10:25 ("The proven one is the foundation of the world"), was elevated into the mediator between God and Man. In Hasidism, for which the Zaddik is exemplified by the Baal-Shem and his successors, the Zaddik is the man in whose life and being the Torah is embodied. "The Zaddik is . . . the man who is more intent than other men on devoting his energies to the task of salvation belonging to all men and to all ages, and whose powers, cleansed and unified, are directed toward this one goal. . . . In him the 'lower' earthly man brings to realization his prototype, the cosmic, primordial man, who encompasses the spheres. In him the world turns back to its origin. He bears the lower blessing upward and brings the higher blessing down. He draws the holy spirit down to men. The Zaddik's being acts upon the upper realms." But he who is content to serve in solitude is not a true Zaddik. Man's bond with God is proven and fulfilled in the human world. The Zaddik gives himself to his disciples (several of whom he usually takes into his household) in transmitting to them the Teaching. He gives himself to his congregation in communal prayer and instruction and as a guide to their lives. Finally he gives himself as comforter, adviser, and mediator to the many who come "travelling" to him from far and wide, partly in order to dwell for a few days—especially on the high Holidays—in his proximity, "in the shade of his holiness," partly in order to obtain his help for the needs of their bodies and souls.